ONE HAND UPON ANOTHER

Given by the
Women's Auxiliary of
the Salvation Army

ONE HAND UPON ANOTHER

by SALLIE CHESHAM

THE SALVATION ARMY • NEW YORK, NEW YORK

ONE HAND UPON ANOTHER, COPYRIGHT © 1978 BY THE SALVATION ARMY. ALL RIGHTS RESERVED. NO PART OF THIS BOOK MAY BE REPRODUCED IN ANY FORM, EXCEPT FOR BRIEF QUOTATIONS, WITHOUT THE WRITTEN PERMISSION OF THE SALVATION ARMY, 145 W. 15TH STREET, NEW YORK, NEW YORK 10011. EASTERN TERRITORY LITERARY BOARD
ISBN 0-89216-016-0

PRINTED IN U.S.A.

The Governor of the Commonwealth of Puerto Rico

FOREWORD

Although the Salvation Army was established in Puerto Rico only relatively recently, it has nevertheless earned a reputation that has brought it ever greater recognition with each passing year.

The men and women who devote their lives to the Salvation Army's good works have made a profound impression upon Puerto Rican life. They have set a superb example for others to follow. And they have brought a measure of comfort and hope to the lives of many of our most forlorn citizens.

To a society which traces its roots back to Christopher Columbus' second voyage of discovery in 1493, an organization whose local history dates back only to 1961 may not seem worthy of much notice. Yet the Salvation Army, founded in Puerto Rico under the direction of Major Tobias Martinez through a commission from General Frederick Coutts, has become one of our deeply valued community institutions.

On behalf of the people of Puerto Rico, I am therefore most pleased to extend warm congratulations and sincere thanks to the Salvation Army, both here and around the world, for the spirit of Christian love and brotherhood that is reflected daily in the actions of its personnel.

Carlos Romero-Barceló

Author's Note

The writing of *One Hand upon Another* has been a sparkling, if provocative, joy, for I have discovered the pioneer Salvation Army marching once again. Living history often is too busy to be interviewed properly and I have been irked that better records have not been kept, that more memories are not visual, and that the whole world cannot hear the "hallelujahs!" that resound from far-away corners despite poor vision, faulty human intention and action, and loneliness. We are as far away from these comrades as they are from us—and I keep longing for a world-circumferential linking of hands. My Lord Jesus taught that that is how the Kingdom of God is to be accomplished, relying upon His indwelling Spirit for guidance.

The Salvation Army was raised up to be God's vanguard of love on the world's battlefield of need. *One Hand upon Another* is not interpretive but reportorial; the former will have to wait until the principals have reached the Golden Strand; but in one sense, the scenes interpret themselves when viewed through time's spectacles. May *One Hand upon Another* comfort and invigorate Christian soldiers who read it, and warn would-be aggressors that both the battlefield and the victory belong to the Eternal.

I am especially grateful to Colonel John Waldron, former Eastern Territorial Chief Secretary, for his vision and support concerning this Caribbean story; and to my husband, "the Colonel," for his continuing patience and assistance in my literary and journalistic ventures—results of the motivation of God's Holy Spirit, I believe.

—*Sallie Chesham*

Contents

I.	OPEN FIRE!	13
II.	ESTABLISH BEACHHEADS	37
	PONCE	58
	LA PERLA	66
	REGIONAL LEADERSHIP	73
	UNITED STATES VIRGIN ISLANDS	81
III.	REVIEW TROOPS	97
IV.	MARCH ON!	131
APPENDICES		
	DEFINITION OF SALVATION ARMY TERMS	139
	"FIRSTS" IN PUERTO RICO AND THE VIRGIN ISLANDS	147
	OFFICERS STATIONED IN PUERTO RICO	151
	BIBLIOGRAPHY	153
	INDEX	155

Little Slum Dog of San Juan

Little slum dogs of San Juan
Wander bonily
Among the sticky,
Stinking steeps
Of La Perla,
And decay

Under balconied calles
In the old walled city,
Eyes down from frowning
Kodak tourists
Who murmur,
"What a pity."

One canine derelict
Guiltily glanced at me.

Surprised,
I realized
That he squandered
Not a wiggle
Nor enjoyed
One glad giggle,
Barking,
Scarcely scratched

His reddened underside,
Widely walking on his
Wooden legs.

Never guessing
That in shellacked
Condominiums
Of nearby Condada,
Bones with red meat
Still attached
Are tossed into hatches
Of incinerators—
Daily.

His eyeing agony
Infested me.
I am become a wondering
Wanderer.
Tell me, is there
Sufficient meat
In any street?
For furtive foundlings?

In any Old San Juan

—Sallie Chesham

Who are these with colors waving,
Sweeping forward through the land,
Toil and strife and danger braving,
Daring for the right to stand?

> *'Tis the Army of salvation,*
> *'Tis the Army of the Lord;*
> *On to conquer every nation,*
> *With the mighty two-edged sword.*

Who are these in town and city,
With their music, song and drum,
Lifting up the name of Jesus,
In the alley, street and slum?

Who are these in love united,
Going forth the lost to win,
Saving souls by evil blighted,
From the depths of grief and sin?

'Tis the Army of salvation,
From the power of sin set free,
Saved from fear and condemnation,
Serving God with liberty!

—ALBERT E. WEBBER

CHAPTER I

Open Fire!

"QUE PASA? QUE PASA? EJERCITA DE SALVACION?"[1]

In Old San Juan's Plaza Colon during a recent Sunday evening, people listened to the Salvation Army street meeting. Not only older residents, tourists and children but also inquisitive, dark-skinned young men questioned. Flags . . . uniforms . . . a loud-speaker . . . brass horns. Singing . . . red ribbons . . . a militant pitch. "Que pasa? Que pasa?"

Some followed to the Army corps hall a half block away on Tetuan Street. Some muttered to companions. Some ignored the singing soldiers as if they were inferior beings.

On a reconnaissance mission also, I wondered—and followed. In two years of wandering, wondering, questioning and reading, this is what I found:

Interest in opening Salvation Army work in Puerto Rico, often called the jewel of the Caribbean, was manifest in 1955, when Lt.-Commissioner George Sandells, Territorial Commander for the Central America and West Indies territory, sent Sr.-Major Tobias Martinez, then commanding Cuba, to conduct a survey concerning

13 . . .

the feasibility of opening Salvation Army work. Martinez believed himself to be the first American of Latin-American descent to be enrolled as a Junior Soldier in the United States.

Martinez reported: "Over one hundred ex-servicemen and women, who had been reached in some way through participation in government activities at Fort Bliss and Fort Kobbe in the Canal Zone, were present to welcome The Salvation Army. Selected men and women representing Protestant churches in Puerto Rico were also present. The Ministerial Association provided a car and driver, used to make the survey . . . Dona Felisa Rincon de Gautier,[2] mayoress of San Juan, entrusted to The Salvation Army a very large Puerto Rican flag which she desired to be laid away with the Army flag that had been taken to Puerto Rico until such time that The Army would start its work in her land." Martinez said that Dona Felisa not only showed a personal interest in The Army coming to her land but promised "every support," her only question being, "Why is The Salvation Army taking so long to come to my land?"

Soon after the survey, Sandells was farewelled and succeeded by Colonel John Stannard, who continued interest in Puerto Rico until informed by International Headquarters that the General would not agree to Puerto Rico being in the Central America and West Indies Territory but that it "would be started through the National Headquarters in the United States, according to a workable plan."

Nothing further was done until shortly after June 28, 1959, when the Martinez family were farewelled from Cuba, returning to the USA Western Territory, their home. Cuba was now communist, the Martinez family had undergone great stress and some privation, and Mrs. Martinez had become ill on the return trip, requiring lung surgery.

Disturbed, restive and painfully conscious of his Latin-American ancestry, Martinez pled with territorial leaders to assign him to Mexico (Mrs. Martinez's birthplace) if he should not be found suitable for an appointment in the United States. He was eager for administrative work, stating in a letter to the National Commander, Commissioner Norman Marshall: "We want to go, if in going we can help advance our forces and help to develop our work. However, we believe there is no point in going if I am to take up some native officer's job, going nowhere and accomplishing little, except to report to work each day and do a few letters or minutes, as was the case in my last appointment in South America East Territory. Please understand my point. I am not complaining, Commissioner; I only wish to point to facts. I am too active, there is too much experience behind me to spend my time in this manner. . . ."

He then suggested that, if he could not be sent to Mexico, he could be allowed to open the work in Puerto Rico, mentioning his survey of 1955.

"The opening of the work in Puerto Rico would be a burden to no one," he wrote the National Commander. "New openings mean new foundations. The required funds to meet the need would be easily secured with the help of a good and solid Advisory Board. Developing the work would mean to take one step at a time, making sure of sound financing, at the same time arousing national interest by meeting certain national needs of the people. There can be certain grants obtained from both governments in Puerto Rico for Salvation Army activities.

"The task of opening Puerto Rico will some day fall upon God's man. That officer must accept the challenge in complete faith. He must be willing to accept the bitter with the sweet. He must be willing to start with nothing. He must be willing to trust God."

A little later he added: "Puerto Rico is an open field . . . an investment of $500 to $1,000 would be all that it would require to open the work there. Only enough funds for a quarters and a building for the first center in San Juan, and within weeks the work would be self-supporting. There is also a great standing force of the armed forces in San Juan. This connection alone offered The Salvation Army $35,000 for the first year of work, from the Armed Forces Community Funds, to open us a center for service personnel. . . ."

The National Commander presented the matter to the Chief of Staff. Colonel Charles Dodd, Chief Secretary for the Western Territory, in acknowledging that notification, wrote: "We have tentatively set aside $10,000 of missionary funds toward this possible opening of Puerto Rico. . . . I do sincerely hope that International Headquarters is prepared to give favorable consideration to the proposal. Perhaps I should say, in closing, that the Commissioner has gone along with the idea of establishing Major Martinez on the basis of his assurance that financing over the long haul would not be a problem and he could take care of the financing of his own work in Puerto Rico."

On December 22, 1960, a letter from the National Commander to the Western Territorial Commander, Lt.-Commissioner Samuel Hepburn, stated: "The General has approved the proposal for Sr.-Major and Mrs. Martinez to open Salvation Army work in Puerto Rico, with the understanding that the Western Territory will underwrite the initial expenses with respect to transporting Sr.-Major and Mrs. Martinez to Puerto Rico and also underwrite the operating costs of this new enterprise for the first year . . . Colonel Dodd informs us that if necessary the West would be willing to cover the cost of the second year also if things did not work out according to the assurance of Sr.-Major Martinez. . . ."

A quick reply reminded the national office that "if you will remember, the Martinezes indicated they could support themselves. However, the West felt somebody would have to assume the responsibility of transportation and agreed to assume this. We also felt that it would be necessary for them to rent a place in which to live and work and they would need some furnishings, etc. Therefore, it was agreed that we would contribute $10,000 toward this venture. Frankly, the Central Finance Council did not have in mind (and neither did the Commissioner) that we would be asked to give more than the $10,000 involved.

"Further, regarding our willingness to do something for the second year, I think this was qualified to the extent that we would be prepared to give 'some assistance' for the second year but, certainly, we were not thinking in terms of another $10,000 particularly in view of the assurances which Sr.-Major Martinez had given. . . ."

A few days later, Colonel Dodd clarified the West's position further, emphasizing the fact that Martinez had given assurance that he could finance the Puerto Rican work, that a survey did not seem necessary, nor did a sponsoring committee, each of which would require more expenditure of money.

"To advance the $10,000 does not mean an indefinite commitment. If the second year required funds (and it would) the West was prepared to consider this eventuality. It would seem only equitable, if this territory financed the first two years, that if further subsidization is needed all the USA territories should be involved. . . .

"You mentioned the development of a social program, etc. plus the cost of building and equipment. If these all have to be underwritten at the onset, the cost can be prohibitive. . . . It seems to me that The Salvation Army should not hesitate to give the Major this opportunity when it appears that he may be able to accomplish this task with an expenditure of $10,000. . . . Another reason for allowing the Martinezes to attempt the opening is that it places loyal Salvationists and loyal Americans in a Latin American situation where both The Army and the United States can use some of this loyalty."

The National Commander believed that a preliminary study and up-dating of the former survey should be conducted "rather than that we should definitely commit ourselves in advance to the opening of Salvation Army work before these factors are determined," and International Headquarters agreed. In February, 1961, the General directed Martinez to proceed alone to Puerto Rico to make a 15-week up-dating survey.

Arriving in Puerto Rico, Martinez hastily reported to the National Commander from San Juan on March 21: "When I was informed . . . that you desired I come alone . . . I argued that already a survey had been made by me, that I saw no need for my family remaining behind or our personal effects not being shipped. . . . I visioned the same Puerto Rico of six years ago, people slowly moving about, and not much activity except on weekends, when hundreds of servicemen would flood the capital. I expected to find a large number of empty buildings and houses for rent . . . the same persons working in the same places and in the same positions. To sum it up, I expected to come and just pick up from where I had left off. How surprised I was to find a new country entwined about the old. Everything was just the opposite from the time the first official survey was made.

"The people of the island are amazed at what is taking place. There seems to be no immediate end to this phenomenal expansion program. The activities on this island seem to me likened to an octopus, an individual, indigenous organization or influence which has far-reaching powers with feelers outreaching in every direction. No one is concerned at the moment about anyone or anything except GOLD.

"I am, however, of the opinion that The Army should consider making the initial investment, even though this would be costly. . . . I am sorry to repeat . . . the interest which could have been in The Army's favor six years ago today has been diverted in other directions.

"It will take a little longer to set up and organize our program and discover new really interested individuals. This is the present obstacle. To date, I have found NO ONE willing to commit himself to give us time. Everyone is coming or going. Each busy about personal gains. Each already active with some other group, or just frankly saying, 'I would not be able to give the time required.' "

"The real cause," he observed another time, "is the new businesses and the large number of persons who are coming in to live for a short period of time. To this add the tourists and you will be able to form a picture of how crowded the island is becoming. . . . Everything you want is in demand, since almost 100% of everything on the island has to get here by imports. . . .

"I have every confidence that within two or three years all of the work that we would have in operation throughout the island would be almost if not entirely self-supporting. . . ."

A short time later, Pedro A. Gonzalez, head of the Commonwealth office in Washington, made a prophetic speech that would have enlightened Sr.-Major Martinez and The Salvation Army even further. Mr. Gonzalez was optimistic as he looked ahead to the future. In part he said:

"The people of Puerto Rico confidently expect to overcome poverty by 1975. In 1940, the people of Puerto Rico awoke in themselves a sort of desperate faith and set in motion a peaceful revolution whose goal was to abolish poverty. If there were no resources, they would import them. If there were no factories, they would create them. Since then a transformation has occurred. There is still poverty, but much less than before. The agricultural economy has become a highly diversified and rapidly expanding manufacturing and agricultural one. The desperate faith has become a faith based on significant tangible achievement. Things which once seemed impossible now appear to be merely difficult.

"The Commonwealth has built schools, hospitals and health centers with unswerving persistence. Schooling is compulsory (and free) through the 16th year . . . English has been compulsory in the schools of this Spanish-speaking island since 1952 (not entirely at the present time). Eighty-six per cent of (the) people are literate (in Spanish). . . ."

During those first weeks Martinez visited business and professional people, preached at the United Evangelical Church to 450 persons and began plans for the first meeting of what he hoped would become a 1,000-member sponsoring committee.

He wrote National Headquarters that Mr. Clyde Page, President of the Christian Business Men's Club, asked that Martinez's superiors be informed that "within the last two or three years several projects had been attempted in the category of service to the people and most of them had folded up, not only for lack of funds but personnel as well," that "The Salvation Army should have full knowledge that the island of Puerto Rico, rated heretofore as only a black dot on the map of the Caribbean, now is the top subject with governments of many countries," and that "what could be done with one dollar three years ago, today would require three."

The Council of Evangelical Churches helped with advice and aired on its weekly program, "Truth and Light," a segment introducing The Salvation Army. The religious press attacked The Army vigorously, for the most part stirring up good will, although some said: "You have no business here . . . Already there are too many queer religions in this country!"

With tempered elation Martinez wrote the national office that he'd finally succeeded in having an interview with San Juan's mayoress, the beloved Dona Felisa Rincon de Gautier, head of mayors and island administrator, living patron saint of Puerto Rico, and known as the leader with the "hand of iron and heart of gold."

Now, though still cordial as in 1955, Dona Felisa made it clear that, in Martinez's words: "We would need to prove ourselves to the people with our work, before assurance could be forthcoming from her city government. If it proved that our work was being done for the people's good and to meet a need, there would be no question that our work would receive every consideration for financial support. But being a new operation, that would be the requirement of the people and it was the people whom she was serving."

"And what kind of work could The Salvation Army do that

19 . . .

would meet a present need?" Martinez asked.

"I wish you would do something for my working boys," she said, "and the man on the street who has no money or no roof over his head at night. Then there is the pressing need to do something for my old people (many of them street beggars). A nice place where some of them can have a clean place to live and feel that they are still human beings. . . ."

On July 3 Martinez recounted a vehement battle between some religious leaders and the Puerto Rican government. This also concerned The Salvation Army, which was directly opposed in print. Martinez noted the confrontation and the general confusion of the people. "Great numbers are leaving themselves open for the gospel of the Lord Jesus Christ."

Of the Army's immediate involvement in the problem, he reported: "The attack on The Salvation Army has done us much good. We have suffered no ill-will from it. In fact, it has tended to strengthen our stand in the nation. It focused the attention of many who otherwise would not have noticed our arrival."

However, in another letter he observed, "Remarks from the general public have not always been good wishes or complimentary as one moves about in Salvation Army uniform . . ."

It was soon apparent that the projected $10,000 cost for one year's operation was extremely unrealistic. Martinez wrote the National Chief Secretary, Lt.-Commissioner Llewellyn Cowan, on April 14, 1961: "I have my doubts that very much of anything, with regard to property, could be purchased for $60,000 in San Juan, and much less in its surrounding suburbs . . . during the second year it would be expected that aside from the income from the institutions in operation, other income would be redeeming our funds from sources within the island. By the end of the second year, plans would already be underway to launch the first financial drive for funds—beginning the third year, from which time, the work already in operation, plus new proposals, would be the sum to be raised in the drive for funds. . . ."

For general publicity and hoping partly by this means to form his sponsoring committee, Martinez distributed cards on which he explained the purpose of The Salvation Army and listed the following most urgent needs it hoped to help meet:

1. Rehabilitation center and chapel for alcoholics;
2. Residence for the aged;
3. Hostel for working lads;
4. Night shelter for homeless men;
5. Community roof garden;
6. Crystal chapel on the roof (for servicemen and public).

The target date for the first sponsoring committee meeting was set for May and Martinez was ready in a hotel room with speech, slides and more printed materials. Due to a heavy rain, only eight citizens attended. A second meeting was planned to which 18 responded. A third was called for and this time the sponsoring committee got underway. The eight persons who attended the first meeting are:

> Victor P. Colon, federal employee
> Miguel A. Jimenez, hotel manager
> Samuel E. Lugo, doctor
> Baldomera Reyes, housewife
> Julio Santiago, ambulance driver
> Mrs. Petra Santiago, practical nurse
> William Fred Santiago, lawyer
> Samuel J. Velez Santiago, university chaplain

Doctor Lugo acted as temporary secretary, and William Fred Santiago acted as temporary chairman and discussion leader. Both were outstanding Christian leaders.

At the first official meeting (three meetings later), Dr. Lugo recorded the minutes, Webster Pullen, President of the First National City Bank of New York, and Benjamin Santana, secretary of the Government Press, chaired the meeting.

Reported Martinez: "Mr. Pullen believes that The Salvation Army will have no problems here with finance, once our National Headquarters shows good faith in making the initial investment in the country to get the work started right. He feels that starting at a very high level will mean our success or failure. Everything that is starting here is top planning all the way, that The Army cannot consider opening unless it is able to make a good investment at the

21 . . .

beginning. He says no one worth anything will want to be connected with us otherwise."

On March 28, he added: "... In my opinion, to start our work in Puerto Rico today would require an investment of no less than $40,000, for installation in the country, from sources outside the island. This would give us a corps hall, an institution and living quarters, all within one building. . . .

"It would cost at least one-half of the initial cost to operate the second year from sources outside the island. I strongly believe, however, that the work in Puerto Rico, regardless of the number of centers it may have in operation on the island, would be self-supporting after the second year. By that time we will have merited the good will and admiration of the people . . . The total cost for a period of two years would not exceed $60,000."

Concerning the eventual territorial responsibility for Puerto Rico, Martinez had noted in his first correspondence on the matter that in 1955 people had questioned him somewhat warily. "What was our plan? They knew that I had come to make the survey from Cuba. What was the connection? . . I made it known that Cuba (as Puerto Rico would possibly be) was a part of 12 countries that made up the Central America and West Indies Territory, that our Territorial Headquarters was in Kingston, Jamaica . . . Ministers, industry, government would have none of that. If The Salvation Army of Puerto Rico was to have an outside headquarters it would be the United States."

On June 15, 1961, the National Commander wrote to Commissioner Owen Culshaw, International Secretary for the Americas, "The Eastern Territory has invested $25,000 for repairs, alterations, equipment and furnishings. . . . I recommend that the work be placed under direction of the Eastern Territory (USA). . . .

"On this same point let me suggest that it would be fatal at this time to attempt to merge the work in Puerto Rico with the West Indies and Central American command. The situation in Puerto Rico is, as you know, quite different from that in Cuba . . . Puerto Ricans enjoy full privileges as citizens of the United States and therefore the administrative control should come under the United States and as indicated before, the Eastern Territory is both willing and able to undertake the assignment. . . ."

International Headquarters informed the national commander on July 6 that "this letter should be attached to the Eastern Territory MOA (memorandum of appointment)" . . . "You will now be held responsible for our work in Puerto Rico. It is agreed that the work shall be officially opened September of 1962 and from that date onwards and until it shall be otherwise decided, the supervision and control of the work there shall be the responsibility of the Territorial Commander for the USA Eastern Territory."

On July 5, 1961, Martinez excitedly wrote National Headquarters, stressing his despondency over the inability to procure a building (intended for headquarters, corps, program for the aged and servicemen's center) because permission had been tardy and now the first floor of that building had been rented to a nightclub. He proceeded:

"Late Monday night I received a telephone call from a gentleman. He wanted to come and see me. He did, and on Tuesday he and his wife came for me at the hotel. They have something fantastic to offer The Salvation Army . . . He said that by chance he read the ad. His eyes fell on The Salvation Army. He knew he had the answer to his prayer, for he had been speaking with several individuals and groups since a week ago when classes finished, about his plans to change his line of business . . . It has been seven years that his Academia Rovira has been in operation (kindergarten through fourth grade), serving the precious youth of his country. His name is Jose J. Rovira, his private school bears his name. His school is accredited, approved and properly registered. . . .

"We are in sight of everything we need, and nothing more need be granted for the projects already outlined in our handbill, but the center that will make all this possible will be the private (Christian) school. . . .

"The entire school will be turned over to us for $500 each month, all of the equipment included. The only extra requirement will be that the rent be paid one year in advance . . . We cannot go wrong with this offer; to let it slip by would be a terrible loss. . . ."

On July 7, Colonel William Harris, Chief Secretary for the East, observed to his superior: ". . . Martinez proposes we take over a coeducational school for infants, capacity 300 with four teachers. His idea is that it would pay for itself, and we could use the building

Saturdays and Sundays for corps purposes. It was a last minute thought with very little data. We hardly considered it. . . . Colonels Slater and Stimson are flying to Puerto Rico on Tuesday, July 11."

Apparently, reconsideration was almost immediate, for the minutes of the Eastern Territorial Property Board on July 28 mentioned purchase of two buildings in Puerto Rico on July 25. "One is a children's shelter for 'lower middle-class children' accommodating 250 children at a cost of $36,000; in addition to this approximately $5,000 will be invested in installing a cafeteria. This will be a source of considerable income"

The minutes also mentioned the purchase of "a second downtown (property) four stories and a roof garden. It was anticipated that the work (located at 353 Tetuan Street in Old San Juan) would be subsidized for 18 months or two years but that it would then be self-sustained."

On July 30, Martinez assured National Headquarters that "within a year from the date of opening, no less than 10 or 12 other centers should be started." In another letter he exulted that "there can be a great harvest . . . The Salvation Army will be able to establish no less than three good divisions, with no less than 30 centers of work in each." Martinez further stated that he was "well prepared to tackle this situation (school at Caparra Terrace) as I have been involved with the operation of private schools for The Army in other lands," and said that Mr. Rovira would remain with The Army for a reasonable time to make the transition smooth.

The budget estimate at that time was $45,435.30.

Regarding the need to understand the Puerto Rican culture, Martinez at this time commented: "Though Puerto Rico is a commonwealth state, a possession of the continental US, the capital influenced by the American way of life, it cannot at any time be considered in the same light as any part of the continental US. Puerto Rico, regardless of how much dressing up it gets, will always be a Latin American country, and there will be need to accept it on those terms from the very beginning . . . will be changed very little, within its native heart, even though from afar off it may look like a suburb of continental United States. . . ."

The school, located on Lot 19, Caparra Terrace in nearby Rio Piedras and formerly called Academia Rovira, would now be renamed Academia William Booth. On request, two new 48-passenger buses were contributed by the Eastern Territory, painted yellow with red borders, with the name of the school on each side, plus Army shields in Spanish and English. A third bus, inherited from the original owner, was blue.

Late in September, 1961, Colonel Paul Carlson, Eastern Territorial Financial Secretary, visited Puerto Rico, suggesting in his report that the projected Harbor Light corps program be set aside for a family corps because of changing conditions in Tetuan Street, including the removal of "two vice-packed places and the moving of the harbor area to another area about 5-6 miles away toward which alcoholics are gravitating."

"Tetuan Street," he said, "is one of the oldest and main streets of activity in Old San Juan. The specific portion where our building is located is largely that of warehouses (tobacco) and commission merchants. Future plans call for a movement of these businesses away from this street and their replacement by shops which will draw tourists. . . ." Noting that he had observed that there did not seem to be residences in the locale, he was told by Martinez that "there are families in second-stories of the present buildings."

Regarding the Academia William Booth, he reported: "Despite repeated promises by Mr. Rovira that he would arrange for a proper transfer by the Department of Instruction for Puerto Rico of the school program in the name of J. Rovira to The Salvation Army, this transfer has not been effected since the school property came into the possession of The Salvation Army on August 29 . . . This is only one of the unsatisfactory experiences with which the Major has had to cope in his dealings with both Mr. Rovira and his wife.

"Very little attention has been given by Mr. Rovira since he sold the property to The Salvation Army. An evidence of this lack of responsibility, despite his assurances that he would assist the Major and see him through to January 31, 1962, is the small enrollment of 62 children as compared with the 250 students projected in the income budget submitted by Colonel Stimson based on detailed estimates submitted by Mr. Rovira.

". . . Mr. Rovira had accepted fees from pupils for the first month, beginning September 18, but retained the income . . . the income to date is not sufficient to meet commitments for teachers' salaries and other expenses. . . . This is primarily due to the small enrollment of 62 pupils as compared with the anticipated enrollment of 250 pupils needed to produce the excess of income over expense of $14,640.00. . . .

"Of the 62 pupils, only 23 have paid in full, leaving 39 who have not paid in full. . . . Quite obviously, Sr.-Major Martinez faces a very unsatisfactory financial situation; however, he expressed confidence that 100 more enrollments could be secured within the next two weeks. . . . If Martinez is successful . . . it will ease the financial situation somewhat but not enough to avoid the need for an advance of funds to the school to discharge financial obligations which exceed available income at this point. . . ." Rovira resigned almost immediately, and soon after Martinez thanked the Eastern Territory through Colonel Carlson "for being involved for the moment, and for the next three years, when by that time we hope our work is well established among the people and self-supporting. We will carry out each of the proposed plans, especially the four cities that will need to be opened by the first anniversary . . ."

Now came a new problem. Willful resistance and vandalism jeopardized the academy, and Martinez wrote home: "I will now need help, the school cannot operate unless it is guarded every operation hour. We have encountered evil-minded individuals. We must protect the Army's interest for the immediate present at our academy, until such time that certain things pass away and we establish on our own merit. I cannot keep on this kind of alert, requiring almost round-the-clock alertness, and expect to be at so many places and meet so many people. . . ."

Response from headquarters was immediate. On November 15, 1961, from the USA Eastern Territory came Captain and Mrs. Richard Shaffstall with their two children Richard and Eric. He was to become school administrator for the Caparra Terrace school which would now be known as the William Booth Academy (opened February, 1962).

They became part of the group which conducted the first Salvation Army indoor meetings on the island, held in the kindergarten room of the Academia. The first meeting was a prayer service on November 16, which 12 people attended, including Martinez, the Shaffstalls with their two children and Brigadier Herbert Sparks, who was visiting the island on behalf of the Territorial Property Department. It was an informal meeting, including a chorus; a prayer led by Shaffstall; a vocal quartet message, "I'd Rather Have Jesus," by the academy bus driver, Mr. Pelley, his wife and two friends; and a request for prayer for a very ill mother by the father of one of the academy children. Sparks gave a testimony message and Martinez closed in prayer.

The following Sunday schedule included Sunday school, holiness meeting, open-air service and salvation meeting. All of these were led by Martinez except for the salvation meeting, which was led by the Shaffstalls, the Bible message being presented by the bus driver, Mr. Pelley.

Shaffstall was shocked at the run-down condition of the school facility. The four classrooms would make one good-sized living room. There was no boys' washroom, and the girls', in which there were two toilets in a tiny closet, had a roof which leaked badly. Something would have to be done.

The second week after his arrival, Shaffstall was told by Martinez, "You're on your own from now on as far as meetings are concerned." The Shaffstalls, with their two sons, distributed meeting announcements in Spanish to every house in the neighborhood and Shaffstall preached in English on Sunday to an uncomprehending crowd of curious Puerto Ricans. He was disconcerted and so were they; however, at the conclusion of the meeting he read in careful Spanish (having been coached by an aide at the Spanish language center) an invitation to accept Jesus Christ as Savior and Lord. Five people walked up the aisle. He motioned to them to kneel, horrified to realize that he could not explain the way of salvation—nor anything else, and praying, "Lord, You got me into this. Don't let these people lose out because I'm not prepared!" For the next three months these folk plus several others accompanied the Shaffstalls to open-air meetings, speaking on the portable unit microphone contributed by WOR-TV engineer Robert Barkey. Three months later, Shaffstall was able to understand what his converts had been saying: they were witnessing to their conversion. One, a kindergarten teacher in the academy, very soon directed a morning chapel service and helped many children receive Christ.

Shaffstall felt he must do something about the school duplex,

27 . . .

and there were two immediate needs: telephone and electricity. The telephone company told him service replacements were behind three years, as did the electric company. The Army would have to wait its turn. Shaffstall went exploring. There was a transformer on a pole a block and a half away. An electrical supply company representative told him what kind of wire he would need to bring electricity from the transformer to a fuse box and sold him the wire. He went back, "climbed the pole and strung the wire to the school, hooked on to the fuse box at the school and then hooked the wires on at the transformer, wired the school building for lights and turned on the switches. Light!" Three years later the electric company came as promised, put in a meter and began sending bills.

Shaffstall then engineered construction of two habitable facilities, with the help of a mason and men who worked for the city every other month, and on their off months worked for The Army in exchange for food. They knocked out a six-foot wide retaining wall, took out 83 truckloads of dirt by wheelbarrow, then built six classrooms, four washrooms, a lunchroom, offices and chapel, two carports, a play area for school and corps and prepared for the second-floor area. Construction costs for school and corps property amounted to $59,630.[3] The corps grew beyond the chapel walls, until Sunday school had to be conducted in the playground, and enrollment in the academy increased appreciably; when Shaffstall arrived he'd found 23 children enrolled with only 18 attending; when he was farewelled in August of 1962 to open fire in Ponce, there was an enrollment of more than 100. Shaffstall commented in his Brief:

"The possibilities at the school are tremendous and we are grateful indeed for the privilege that was ours of being able to serve in the school even for such a brief period of time. We are confident that the future of the school will be a bright one and that the blessing of God and the extension of His Kingdom will be in evidence day by day and year by year."

When Brigadier Freda Weatherly reached Puerto Rico on June 27, 1962, to become the island's first Financial Secretary, she especially noted the efforts of the Shaffstalls at Caparra Terrace and the William Booth Academy: "I was immediately impressed by the Shaffstalls' deep concern for the people and their willingness to do anything to help the program there. For the Captain, this often meant many hours of hard work in keeping up with the repair work on the building and also cleaning the grounds for the erection of a new building. When they were transferred to Ponce to open the work there, the same concern and zeal was evident."

The first Puerto Rican Home League met on May 7, 1962, at Caparra Terrace, with an enrollment of ladies on July 3 and 8. Thirteen Junior Soldiers were enrolled at Caparra in June, 1962.

Reliance on God's leading resulted in scores of meaningful experiences for the Shaffstalls. The following is no exception.

From a newspaper editor Shaffstall received a letter addressed: "To whom it may concern." It came from a lady in New Jersey who said she had a cousin in the mountains on the northwest shore near Baranquitas who was paralyzed from his waist down and had no way of getting around. Shaffstall decided to visit him.

He found the home, an 8 x 10 room on stilts. The 42-year-old cousin was dragging himself about by his arms on the floor. He made his own living, having learned to fell trees from a lying-down position, and sold the wood to neighbors for groceries. He'd never been in a store. A little later, Shaffstall took the man a wheelchair, accompanied as interpreter by the "best English speaker" in the academy, 4th-grade student Richard, who'd been abandoned as a baby.

A crowd gathered to view the wheelchair presentation, and Shaffstall couldn't resist conducting an open-air service, singing choruses and telling the story of the unseen Friend who cares about everyone and had brought him here. His interpreter looked skeptical, but as he repeated after the Captain the meaning of the Crucifixion, he turned, weeping, and said, "You mean He cares for me? Is it true He did it for me?"

"Yes," Shaffstall said. "He did."

While the crowd watched and listened, the conversation continued.

"Can I know Him like you do?"

"Yes."

"When?"

"Now." The Captain then had Richard ask if others would like to receive the Divine Presence into their lives and several raised their hands. Recounts Shaffstall: "I led Richard to Christ in prayer and he then led the others. The beauty of the complete silence on everyone's part while this was going on made us all aware something miraculous was taking place."

On January 15, 1962, Martinez conducted his first meetings at the renovated Tetuan Street building. The day before, Shaffstall installed lights so the meetings could be held on the second floor as the first floor allotted to the San Juan Temple Corps was not ready.

Then on February 22, 1962, with the flags of Puerto Rico, the United States and The Salvation Army waving together over the building at 353 Tetuan Street in the walled city of Old San Juan (still architecturally reminiscent of Spanish colonial days, and now a mecca for tourists), The Salvation Army was officially opened in Puerto Rico.

From New York City came Commissioner Holland French, Territorial Commander, accompanied by other Army leaders and the New York Staff Band ensemble. They were joined on the island by leading citizens headed by Mayoress Dona Felisa Rincon de Gautier, military officials and the 81st U.S. Army band. Dona Felisa, being made the first auxiliary member of The Army in Puerto Rico, urged her people to "accept The Army and open its arms," and the chorus, "How Great Thou Art!" was sung in both Spanish and English. Of the official opening, Commissioner French stated to General Wilfred Kitching: ". . . We had large crowds with many prominent people attending the official opening service, and quite a number of seekers. I was privileged to enroll one junior soldier, two senior soldiers and eight recruits. There is a wonderful opportunity in Puerto Rico for The Army. We can expand into other areas, with corps, as quickly as we can find people and funds. . . ."

Prominent guests attending the celebration service included:

    Miss Carmen Ongay (University of Puerto Rico)
    Antonio H. Bennazar
    Aaron Holman
    Rev. Antonio Rivera Rodriquez (Secretary, Council of Churches)
    Rev. Donald E. Johnson
    Commandante Ernesto Lugo Mendez (Police, Capitol District)
    Senador Arturo Ortiz Toro
    Dr. and Mrs. Samuel Lugo

Mrs. Mercedes Velez de Perez
Mr. Agustin Vera Palma
Dr. Carlos Lastra
Chaplain (Major) Richard E. Robinson (Antilles Chaplain)
Chief of Staff, Colonel James D.C. Breckenridge (Antilles Command)
Honorable Mayoress Dona Felisa Rincon de Gautier (Mayoress of San Juan)
Mrs. Estela Maria Davila Lanauze
Colonel Rafael Montilla (Army ROTC, University of Puerto Rico)
Ledo Juvenla Rosas
A.W. Maldonado
E. Combas Guerra
Hector Modeste
Chaplain William S. Noce (USN—US Naval Station, San Juan)
Rev. Rafael Angel Maldonado
Rev. Gildo Sanchez
Ing. Jorge J. Jimenez
Captain Ruben O. Figueroa (Army ROTC, University de Puerto Rico)
Ex. Teniente Alejandro Oliveras
Gunter Hatt
Pedro Burgos
J. Joseph McIntyre (Robinson School)
Pedro Javier Bosio, Centro Universitario

The international Salvation Army, committed by its founder William Booth, who believed it was God-raised, to reach arms of love around the world, had marched into Puerto Rico, flags flying, drums beating, bands playing, soldiers singing.

Now what?

Notes

1. Translation: "What's happening, Salvation Army?"

2. She first became interested in The Salvation Army when meeting the present Commissioner Hjalmar Eliasen during a social welfare conference held in Puerto Rico.

3. Approved by Territorial Headquarters Property Board May 19, 1964.

Opening Ceremonies in Puerto Rico

Commissioner Holland French presenting the Mayoress of San Juan, Dona Felisa de Gautier, special Salvation Army garland as a memento of the historic occasion which saw initiation of the organization's multiphased work in Puerto Rico.

*Opening Ceremonies
in
Puerto Rico*

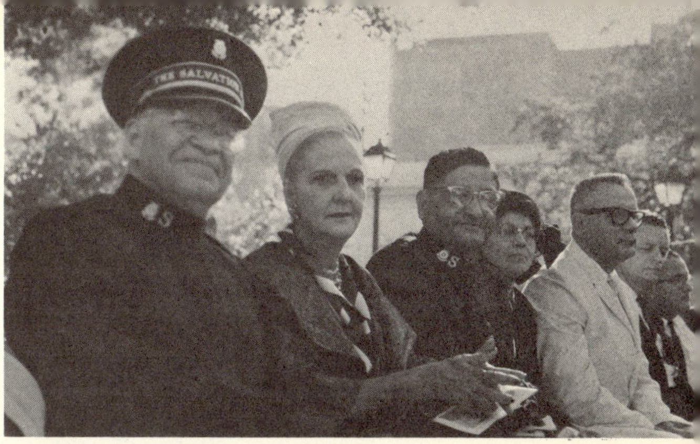
THE SALVATION

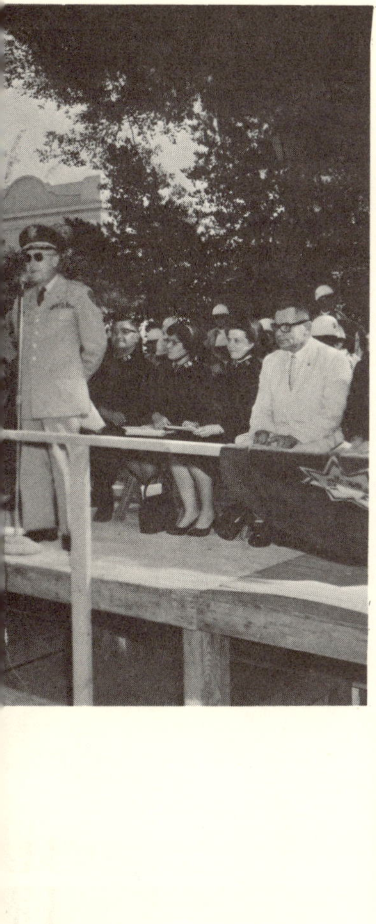

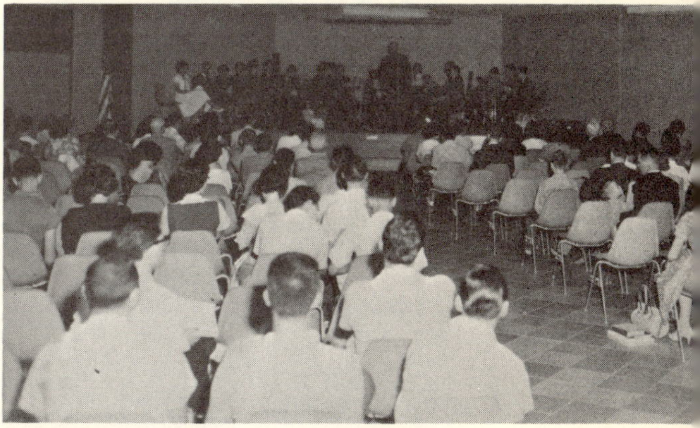

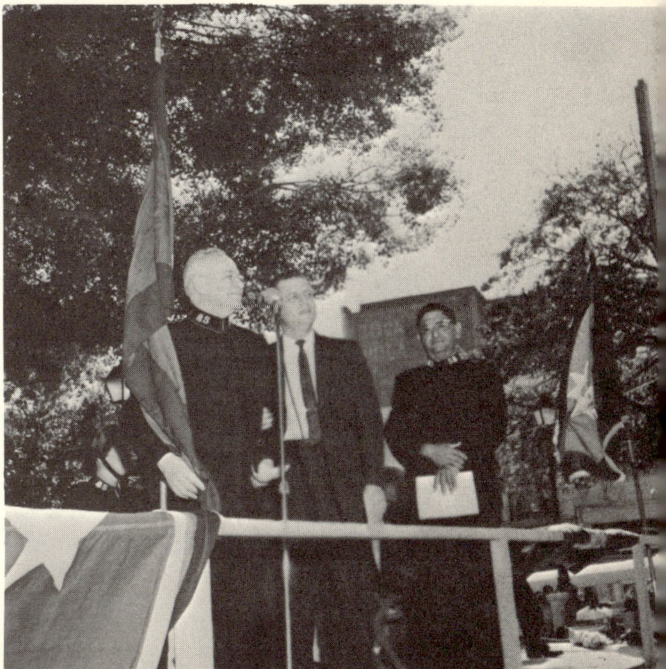

Come, join our Army, to battle we go;
Jesus will help us to conquer the foe,
Fighting for right and opposing the wrong;
The Salvation Army is marching along.

>*Marching on, marching along;*
>*The Salvation Army is marching along;*
>*Soldiers of Jesus, be valiant and strong;*
>*The Salvation Army is marching along!*

Come, join our Army, and do not delay,
The time for enlisting is passing away;
Fierce is the battle, but victory will come;
The Salvation Army is marching along.

—WILLIAM PEARSON

CHAPTER 11

Establish Beachheads

The initial Salvation Army work in Puerto Rico included the already thriving Caparra Terrace corps, the Academia William Booth at the same location, and the San Juan Temple corps housed in the first floor of the Tetuan Street property. Regional headquarters and the general office were located on the second floor and a senior citizens' residential center was planned for the third floor. Plans were also under consideration for a roof garden, to include rest, recreation and informal worship accommodations. A men's hotel and an institute of languages were also being considered.

Set in the middle of the tobacco warehouse-dock district in Old San Juan, the Tetuan Street building did not appeal as an Army center to many who discussed its suitability. The neighborhood was not residential, most standing buildings were to be torn down in an urban renewal program, (although in fact, this has not happened), and the building itself was not in good condition. These facts, in part, prohibited the realization of the senior citizens' center and roof-top garden for servicemen. A men's hotel, situated about a block and a half away from headquarters and called Hope House, was closed in

1970 as a more comprehensive work of service to men was begun at the Caparra Terrace property as part of a multi-faceted social welfare program called the Multiplex Welfare Center. The first year's proposed operating budget for Puerto Rico was $18,696.00.

In June of 1962 Brigadier Freda Weatherly was appointed to Puerto Rico as Regional Financial Secretary. Her first responsibility was to establish financial and statistical records from the time of the commencement of the work. Because there was only a set of loose-leaf pages and a fairly large number of bills and vouchers, most of which were in Spanish, this proved a monumental task, especially because she knew no Spanish. "However," she later recalled, "with the help of a good dictionary in both languages, the records were set up and the reports sent off to Territorial Headquarters."

Also in June, Captain and Mrs. Bernard Smith arrived to assist the now Brigadier and Mrs. Martinez and pioneer the work at San Juan Temple corps (not to be confused with the Caparra Terrace school-corps operation which was directed by Captain and Mrs. Shaffstall). They had served in South America, spoke fluent Spanish and were forthright and aggressive. After the official opening, meetings had been conducted in the Tetuan Street building and five soldiers had been enrolled under the leadership of Candidate Virginia Martinez, but the grueling groundwork remained to be done.

Many difficulties had to be overcome. Smith recalls: "In the corps we had few, if any furnishings. We had problems with the electricity. The building really was not ready for use as a corps." Another important factor was that the Smiths had nowhere to live and, with their two children, were crowded into a single room in the Robinson School for several weeks. The quarters assigned to them eventually, was a long distance from the corps, and commuting was time-consuming and tiring with two small children and an accordion, the only means of music.

Open-air meetings, door-to-door visitation and cottage meetings were emphasized with the Smiths holding at least three open-air meetings weekly in nearby Plaza Colon. "We never were without a crowd," states Smith. "People would listen attentively and many souls sought Christ at the drumhead or followed us to the hall and accepted Christ in the indoor meeting."

Among those open-air converts was Mrs. Carmen Marzan, still a faithful worker, and the present Corps Sergeant-Major, Isaac Del Valle, who remains enthusiastic about outdoor services and has a most distinctive and robust manner of giving announcements in meetings, stating God's claims in strong language. In the autumn of 1963 Del Valle had been strolling one Sunday evening in Plaza Colon with his small daughter Margarita when they heard adventurous, bombastic speech.

"Daddy!" urged Margarita, "those people are talking about Jesus. Let's go listen!"

They listened to the Smiths' enthusiastic message of Jesus who, they declared, that very night walked in some mysterious and miraculous way on the plaza, peering over the shoulders of doting domino players, weeping over balding, bawdy prostitutes, stringy sad beggars—even the emaciated little street dogs who trotted from crevice to corner, tilting expectant ears.

The Del Valles followed the Salvationists to the hall and immediately became interested in Christ's militant claims as Salvationists presented them. "We are saved to serve!" was the message. "Salvationists consider the world God's battlefield. We must win the lost and sinful, the sick and the sorrowing. God cares about them! We are the soldiers of Jesus' love and glory!"

Del Valle liked that kind of talk. And so did Margarita. She became a winning and demanding recruiter, bringing other children almost every time she attended services (from Old San Juan where the family lived). Eventually she brought her irrepressible, quick-witted cousin, Iris De La Rosa, and Iris's father. Iris is now an officer and her father a uniformed soldier. In this person-to-person manner The Army went from victory to victory, though, as in all battles there were many who, finding the discipline too exacting, the fighting too rigorous, the challenge too exhausting, gave up—or were overwhelmed by the enemy.

The first Christmas effort in Puerto Rico was directed and effected by the Smiths in 1962, she playing her accordion and he his trombone. Though the amount raised was modest, with it many families were cheered, especially in La Perla, the destitute area of Old San Juan.

Soon after the beachhead had been made secure, the Martinezes were transferred to the mainland. On January 30, 1963, Major and Mrs. Eldred Churchill, seasoned and compassionate officers of many years' service were appointed Regional Commanders. They were immediately confronted with several major tasks: to commence new outreach programs; tackle the problems of operating the William Booth Academia at Caparra Terrace; deal with the San Juan corps operation; establish a solid financial foundation on the island; handle other requests from various sources; and to do something about the pressing need for an Advisory Board of island leaders.

The Churchills learned that the wife of the Caribbean manager of the First National City Bank of New York, Mrs. Webster Pullen (nee Gretchen Swanson of Swanson Frozen Foods) had been a member of the Salvation Army Advisory Board in Omaha, Nebraska. It was arranged that the Churchills visit Mrs. Pullen, who agreed to contact other persons who would act as an organizing committee. A few weeks later another meeting was held, and Major Churchill was introduced to William Waymouth who became the first Advisory Board Chairman for Puerto Rico. The committee selected an impressive group of men and women to be board members, keeping an equal balance of mainland and Puerto Rican citizens, and the first official meeting was held at regional headquarters in August, 1963.

Also, in the first six months of the new year, Major Churchill directed the complete renovation of the San Juan Temple facility which had been in woeful disrepair. The necessary furnishings were acquired and the Smiths were able to carry out the corps program much more efficiently and attractively. "The greatest joy we had in this appointment," recalls Smith, "was to see lives changed and The Army move forward."

On loan from Chile, the Smiths were now eager to return and were granted permission during the summer of 1963. They again served in Puerto Rico from 1966-9, the Captain serving as Regional Secretary. San Juan Temple corps was now without leadership for six weeks, during which Brigadier Weatherly, the Finance Officer, was made responsible for corps activities. It will be remembered that she spoke no Spanish, and neither did the Churchills. To Freda this was a definite drawback, though she felt the Churchills' loving-kindness and ardor compensated to a great extent. The Brigadier determinedly applied herself to the language, being greatly concerned that she could not even converse with her soldiers.

Had it not been for the Home League Secretary (whose efforts had already resulted in a virile Home League), a nurse named Medarda Melendez, the venture would have been impossible. Freda wrote her messages in English and Medarda translated them into Spanish. At the appropriate time in the meeting, Freda would read her message (sermon) which included an altar call. "It's a very strange experience to bring a Bible message and not know what you are saying," she recalls. "For by that time the English translation had been forgotten. As I look back over that experience I wonder how I ever had the courage to do it, and I marvel at the endurance of the people who came every night there was a meeting—which was every night and twice on Sunday—as well as open-airs. God bless Miss Medarda Melendez—wherever she is!"[1]

The determined Brigadier continued her language effort and in following months succeeded in teaching both Bible and Doctrine classes.

Captain and Mrs. Frank Payton, newly appointed corps officers for San Juan Temple arrived in September of 1963. They were mainland officers who had been serving in Argentina for several years. The Paytons spoke Spanish with ease, were orderly and industrious. Frank Payton did not think the men's hotel program was feasible, though he managed it until Christmas in addition to the corps work, when his primary efforts were invested in Christmas fund-raising, by now established as a street-corner kettle operation.

Early in the Paytons' appointment at San Juan Temple, exploratory work was begun in La Perla, a stricken area a few blocks from the corps building on the north shore tip of the Old San Juan peninsula, outside the walls of the old city, and near the historic stone fort. Here, hundreds of families lived in wooden shacks which clustered around the water's edge. La Perla was established about 50 years ago when needy families, many from outlying areas, decided to nest free or with little charge, just outside the city walls. Here miniature houses and shacks cling to the slope that helped protect the Spanish-ruled city from 1493 to 1898, between the wall and the Atlantic Ocean. They rise, one atop another, with communally used ramped concrete walks and steps serving as lawns and thoroughfares.

La Perla is situated between the historic El Morro and San Cristobal castles, where guard houses stand as empty and ancient sentinels of a lurking past, and green-painted roofs still provide protective coloration.

La Perla homes usually have one or two rooms partitioned with drapes, and are painted brightly and ornamented with high-hung religious pictures, tapestries and artificial flowers. There are no gardens, no trees, but there are innumerable doorless cubbyhole-stores like little commercial pantries, with juke boxes pounding out Castillian tunes while La Perlians, tacked to minute porches like fluttering butterflies, hum, chat and watch passersby.

In La Perla, living conditions are very poor. During the last survey conducted by the commonwealth in 1968, it was indicated that more than 40 per cent of the population have no separate bedrooms; almost 40 per cent of couples live consensually; education standards are low, approximately one-fourth of the 25 and older group have not completed first grade; school attendance for children is about 50 per cent; about 20 per cent of population of 14 and over are illiterate. Many La Perlians can't find employment, and most of those who do are unskilled. Incomes are as low as $500 and do not exceed the $4,000 bracket for the more affluent. The 1960 census set the approximate population at 3,300 people living in about 900 housing units. The population now is estimated at about 10,000.

"We began with open-airs," recalls Payton, "and soon were bringing children from there to our Sunday school and Junior Legion programs." Every Sunday afternoon a small group of Salvationists would visit, and every week scores of children were waiting. They were invited to attend craft classes and Junior Legion meetings in addition to the regular Sunday school; soon, 50 to 70 children were attending activities at the corps building. The Paytons then employed a Dominican Christian woman to do visitation in La Perla.

When, in June of 1964, they were transferred to Ponce, Captain and Mrs. Roberto Pagan[2] arrived to become Corps Commanding Officers at San Juan Temple corps. The Pagans worked vigorously in La Perla, conducting both visitation and open-air meetings on a weekly basis. During the same period, work was also begun in the barrio of San Jose in the nearby town of Rio Piedras.

In August of 1962, when Captain and Mrs. Shaffstall were

appointed to open Salvation Army work in Ponce, the second city to be invaded by The Salvation Army in Puerto Rico, Captain Gilberta Hess was appointed as Corps Officer of the Caparra Temple corps, and temporary school administrator (assisting in the corps at this time was Lieutenant Carol Snyder and later, Miss Milagros Pagan). Not long commissioned from the Eastern School for Officers' Training, Captain Hess had enjoyed an appointment at the Spanish-speaking Manhattan Citadel corps and had felt out of place when transferred to other work. She had mentioned this to the Field Secretary, Colonel Albert Pepper, and also the fact that she thought The Army should be in Puerto Rico. He inquired if she would be willing to serve on the island but didn't mention that The Army was considering such an opening.

Now her chance had come. "I was not only thrilled at seeing how God worked," recalls Gilberta, "but also frightened. I'll never forget the day I went to the airport. I cried and cried as we lined up to board the plane and so much wanted to turn and say to my parents, 'I can't do it.' How homesick I felt already. Yet I could not quit, as for the first time I really felt in the center of God's will. There was no turning back."

Arriving at Caparra Terrace, Gilberta was charmed to be met by four little curly-haired boys who sat on the front steps and sang to her. It was not until about two months later that she learned what they were singing:

> "We'll never let this lady captain come,
> Because Captain Shaffstall is the one—
> Who's BOSS here!"

It took some loving and some learning to be received happily. They had loved the Shaffstalls so much. The boys did, however, become close friends and fellow soldiers and one, Lieutenant Eric Diaz, became the Commanding Officer of the San Juan Temple and La Perla corps. Soon, Eric, his brother Ramon and two other young boys climbed into a banana tree every morning and threw stones at the Captain's window to make sure she was up and about her duties.

On arrival, Gilberta was especially intrigued by the little chapel at Caparra. "To me it was just beautiful. Adding to the sense of worship was the knowledge that the benches and pulpit had been constructed by San Juan prisoners."

Again, language proved to be an exasperating problem. When Gilberta was finally brave enough to attempt a sermon in Spanish, it was a complete disaster. She had worked for days on the sermon, but when she attempted to talk about the Star of Bethlehem, she managed only to utter words that, translated, meant "the milk of a hen," and wondered tearfully what had gone wrong when the congregation exploded in laughter. In about six months she could make herself understood and though, in her estimation, her pronouncements must have sounded like children's stories, nevertheless people were won for the Master and grew spiritually, eager to serve in the ranks of The Army.

Aided by her battered old accordion, a sacrificial gift from her parents, Gilberta was much at ease with children; the Sunday school grew rapidly and soon there were 40-50 children attending regularly. Thus, there was no intimation that anything was wrong when one Sunday morning she found no assemblage. Finally, a neighbor told her that a religious person had forbidden the children to attend, warning them that they would all go to hell if they entered the Army chapel again. Gilberta began open-air meetings once more; other children came but also about 75 per cent of the original group filtered back before long.

The children were exhilarating to work with. They learned quickly, sang with gusto and took the discipline of Junior Soldiers of The Salvation Army seriously. Eric and Ramon Diaz were among the first to be enrolled and given "S's" to sew on their shirt collars. Gilberta was saddened but impressed when, about three weeks after the enrollment Ramon Diaz came to her weeping, handed her the "S's" from his shirt and said, "Captain, I'm giving my "S's" to you because I'm not worthy of wearing them." The transgression seemed trifling to Gilberta, but monumental to Ramon.

Intense interest did not come only from children; for example, one sultry night Gilberta led her slender forces to the open-air ring in a residential section. Usually, crowds gathered but this night there was only one listener, a young man. Tired and hot, Gilberta was glad the service was over, but just as she turned to go, the young man asked if he could come to the indoor service. Invited, he brought and

. . . 44

played his flute, inquired about the Salvation Army's purpose and methods and lingered. Ramon Vasquez has been a faithful soldier and employee throughout the intervening years.

During the early days, when Gilberta was acting principal of the academy and still struggling with the language, she yearned to speak fluently, to understand. "Many times," she recalls, "teachers would bring in problem children and chatter something in Spanish. I would just smile and the teacher would walk out, leaving the child. The child would smile and I would smile back. Thankfully, that was a kind of communication. But it wasn't long before I became conversational. I had found my place and felt useful and happy again."

Soon a Torchbearer group was started and in a matter of weeks between 40 and 45 young people met weekly, many becoming Christians. However, one named Betsy worried Gilberta.

A beautiful girl of about 15, she stayed in a corner alone, never joining in. Winning her confidence, Gilberta was told she was being sexually abused by her father. Gilberta talked with her sisters, who were also Torchbearers; they knew, as did the mother. Gilberta gained judicial permission for Betsy to live in the quarters with her, and eventually the father was taken to court and institutionalized.

At Christmastime, Gilberta and her assistant, Lieutenant Snyder, were so homesick they decided to entertain two small orphan girls during Christmas vacation. They contacted the local orphanage and made arrangements. Excitedly they bought dolls and other toys for girls and the day before Christmas they went to greet their little visitors.

"Oh, no!" the girls chorused, "it can't be!" But it was. Their little visitors were two husky boys, 12 and 14 years old. Nothing went right. The boys spoke no English and the girls stumbled along in Spanish. Gifts could not be found that late on Christmas Eve, and the boys were annoyed with American cooking. What to do? In desperation, Gilberta decided to bring in playmates. Eric, Ramon and Richard, some of the banana-tree boys, were invited to visit also. Then the celebration was begun!

Another Christmas Eve was significant but tragically so. The girls were returning home from duties when they saw a man lying in the middle of the street. He was screaming in pain, and the stench was nauseating. They had great difficulty getting him into the car and to the hospital. He gasped that he'd been so drunk at a Christmas party where the celebrants were roasting a pig that he'd fallen into the roasting pit. Nobody had bothered to help him and he'd been staggering in the street for some time. The girls stayed with him until five a.m. on Christmas morning. "I can't count the times we would see people in a horrible condition in the streets and take them home," recounts Gilberta Hess, now Mrs. Carlos Valentin.

Mrs. Major Churchill, wife of the Regional Commander, had established a schedule of institutional visitation, and the League of Mercy activity was one of the first and finest on the island. Gilberta especially enjoyed visits to the tuberculosis hospital for children. "The Churchills were so concerned for children," she recounts. "I was blessed just being with them in their Christlike ministry. I loved visiting the children in the TB hospital, where I would take my old accordion and sing with the other women officers. Though some were terribly ill and many had inflated abdomens from malnutrition, they all listened so attentively to the stories about Jesus, and sang like nobody ever sang before or since! My accordion was almost a playmate to them. They called it the 'symphonia' and were ecstatic when their thin little fingers touched a note, or they tried to play it with me."

Joys and successes outnumbered sorrows and defeats, but the latter were not uncommon — and they are remembered achingly well. A school teacher, Mrs. Monet, became interested and sent her children to Sunday school accompanied by their dignified white-haired grandfather who often gave a most effective testimony. Later, the girls missed him for two or three weeks and upon inquiry were told that he'd moved away but could the Captain come talk to him on Saturday please?

Intentions were the best, but when the girls reached home from hospital visitation late Saturday afternoon, they were exhausted. Lieutenant Snyder said, "Look, Gilberta, we've no groceries. I'll stop by and see what Mr. Monet wants on my way home from the grocery store."

When the Lieutenant reached Mr. Monet's home, he was dead. Suicide. The landlady explained, "He was waiting for Captain all morning but she didn't get here in time."

Captain Hess was asked to conduct Mr. Monet's funeral. "It

was one of the most difficult tasks of my life," she recalls. "I knew I should have gone. I'd felt guilty about not going, but I stayed home anyway."

The Shaffstalls had been farewelled in August, 1962, to open the work in Ponce; thus, assisted by Lieutenant Snyder, Captain Hess directed both school and corps activities until 1963 when Cadet-Lieutenant and Mrs. David Hepburn were sent to Puerto Rico and he became principal of Academia William Booth. After their commissioning in June of 1964, he took on the additional responsibility as corps officer at Caparra Terrace. Captain Hess was transferred to Ponce to assist the Paytons.

Basic objectives concerning the Caparra operation were set by the now Brigadier Churchill and Captain Hepburn: make the school property and facility as practically accommodating as possible; secure full accreditation from the Department of Education in Puerto Rico; complete second-floor construction which would provide corps and school with eight additional classrooms to be used cooperatively by school and corps.

David Hepburn and his wife Daisy divided responsibilities: he was responsible for the academic program, planning of facilities, and finance; she assumed full responsibility for the school's Christian education program. They also sought to incorporate in all publicity and advertisements the fact that the academy was a Christian school and that young people were taught according to the principles of Christian Scripture and the doctrines of The Salvation Army.

The Hepburns had studied a crash course in Spanish during their last six weeks in the New York School for Officers' Training, but now wondered just how they would manage. Crash courses never manufacture creditable conversationalists. David continued to study Spanish in Puerto Rico, and as Daisy commented, "He could play the piano in any language." That helped. Because classes were scheduled to begin three weeks after their arrival, their first duty was to scrub the school in preparation for the opening.

When school opened they were delighted with the general response of the children and their parents, especially to the reception of daily chapel services. In the months and years to come, an important feature of their Scripture story and song teaching was the use of very large colorful visual aids. These had been prepared by Hepburn's sister, Mrs. Betty Hansen, who was recuperating from a lengthy illness. This method is considered by the Hepburns to be an invaluable aid in presenting learning materials.

Later, when Lieutenant Enrique Lalut was appointed to assist them, the Hepburns conducted a one-hour chapel service on Friday. Lalut also helped by teaching the Scriptures in the classroom to fifth and sixth graders. It was novel and awesome to Enrique to introduce boys and girls to Christ at his teacher's desk.

A basic school problem was the fact that the teachers were not under contract and were receiving only $105 a month for full-time teaching. One of the Hepburns' objectives was to see that every teacher in the academy had a university bachelor's degree and a teaching certificate. This was accomplished; the next year salaries were accordingly raised, teachers put under contract and the school accredited with the Department of Education.

Also during 1963 plans were presented to the Puerto Rico Planning Board which issued building permits. The USA Eastern Territory agreed to fund the needed school construction additions. The plans were rejected due to local opposition, which was not at the time directly identified; however, by autumn of 1964 plans were revised, objections removed and the permit was granted. Before the end of 1964 construction of the second floor on both buildings was completed, and eight additional rooms were now available. The Academia William Booth could now offer pre-kindergarten and grades one through six. Each grade now had its own properly qualified teacher. Two Cuban refugee teachers were additionally skilled, one having a master's and one a doctor's degree in education.

Three persons worthy of note during the pioneer days at Caparra Terrace were Danilo Gonzales, a former officer and refugee from Cuba, who gave enthusiastic and skilled support. Contemporaries recall: "He was a big man with a loud voice who had a winning way with children." Another was Yufo Pagan, the driver of the school bus and brother of Captain Roberto Pagan. A pig butcher, Yufo was often vocally and humorously lonesome for his home in the middle of the island, and his pigs. He nevertheless gave outstanding service during the Hepburns' appointment.

During their first year in Rio Piedras, the Hepburns felt the need of having some worship in English for their own children, so they started a front-porch Sunday school in their home barrio of Alta Mesa, having begun to know their neighbors. "We not only had a great fellowship with other overseas ministers," recalls Daisy, "but we became quite involved with our neighbors. David's secretary lived just down the street, our children were happily and joyfully accepted into the playing community, and our red-headed, blue-eyed baby daughter was a source of much delight in this dark-haired community."

From contacts with their neighbors the English-speaking Sunday school was built. Enthusiasm mounted and it was not long before about 30 children crowded the porch, singing, praying, listening to the message of a heavenly Lord who believes little children to be very special. Important commitments were made; for example, the Capo family began to attend Sunday school, comely teen-aged Nivea becoming a glowing Christian and Salvation Army soldier. Nivea and her husband, whom she met in 1968 when he was a member of the SAYSO group which campaigned on the island, became Salvation Army officers. Lieutenant and Mrs. Miguel Lopez have been in command of the Jersey City, N.J. corps.

It was also through the Hepburns' neighbors that the first invitations to the Caparra Terrace Home League were distributed. "I was so happy," remembers Daisy, "when the neighbors responded and came to family night at our Home League, and several from our own street were enrolled as members during the first year."

During 1964 Operation Sharing was begun. This was a collection of packaged and canned goods, mostly from private English-speaking schools or church-sponsored schools. Enough food was collected for 250 boxes and bags, each being distributed with a Spanish New Testament by a Salvation Army soldier who prayed with the recipients and invited them to corps activities and Sunday school. There were many responses, but many neighbors did not attend because they did not think they could "dress right." Through this effort, an outpost Sunday school was started in the barrio of Monacillo where sometimes as many as 150 children and young people gathered to sit on bricks and boards to listen to the Great Story.

Also in 1964 a four-pronged evangelistic crusade was conducted, during which 4,000 homes were visited and many people found God. The first was a 10-day period with the Reverend Castaneda and Danilo Gonzales. The second was in conjunction with a group of young people from New York's Manhattan Citadel corps who, under the direction of Bandmaster David Appleby, paid their own expenses and offered an attractive spiritual-musical message. Next, two cadets were assigned from the New York School for Officers' Training. The language problem was again burdensome, though many children responded through the open-air ministry. Hepburn remembers: "We had more response than we were able to cope with in the first year in charge of Caparra Terrace corps."

During 1964 a young Puerto Rican, Benjamin Pastrana, was commissioned as Caparra Temple's first lay leader (Sergeant-Major) and with his young wife and two children became a faithful and zealous soldier. Jesus Martinez was commissioned Missionary Sergeant and Teddy Garcia, Scoutmaster. Of that period, Hepburn comments: "The most encouraging thing in the corps during 1964 was the response of the people to spiritual matters. They also felt that our school served well in the total program. We had capacity enrollment in 1964, and the children did not miss one day even though the second floor was being constructed above us. Of course, even to begin to explain some of the complications of construction is a major task—dealing with a contractor who speaks no English, and you speak little Spanish, your specifications are in English, of course. Finally, we did complete our building, readjusted our facilities and found them to be very adequate for our school and corps programs."

When the Churchills farewelled in 1965, they noted that the academy was a "wonderful feeder to the corps and was operating at capacity enrollment."

During 1964 the Army joined other evangelical churches in force for a giant parade of witness in downtown San Juan. 12,000 Christians marched and sang songs of thanksgiving.

A remarkable achievement was made by the Caparra Terrace corps in 1965 when the Eastern Territory of The Salvation Army conducted a 10-week Sunday school contest and Caparra won! By the time of the contest, Sunday school was held in the backyard of the academy, having grown completely out of the facility. Still the corps was unable to keep up with the growth so activities were conducted in three locations: one in the facilities of the corps; one in Monacillo barrio; and one in a housing project. Highest attendance was 601 with an average of 350. It remained high after the contest and many people were incorporated into the corps.

The experience was characterized by innovation and hard work, tests and rewards of faith, but also some altogether incredible and uproarious experiences. Such was the incident of the helium balloons. During the contest, David had promised the Monacillo Sunday school children—who attended classes under a house, sitting on bricks and boards—that there would be a great balloon contest. On a designated day they would put messages on the strings of balloons and release them. Then whoever got his returned most quickly would receive a prize.

"We didn't understand how difficult it might be to get helium," recalls Daisy, "especially on Saturday afternoon. We just thought we'd blow up our balloons at a nearby tank."

No helium. Finally, David found a place where he could fill the balloons but not rent nor buy the tank. So over he drove in the corps station-wagon, filled as many balloons as could be stuffed into the wagon and began the ride home, only to discover the balloons were leaking! If there were to be any soaring balloons for Sunday afternoon, the helium would have to be transferred.

"Can you imagine us," says Daisy, "using, of all things, the tube from an enema bag, putting it around the neck of the helium-filled balloons and attempting to force the helium into a larger, sturdier balloon! We did the best we could and ended up with about 175 kids and a few big balloons. David made his portentous announcement, the children tied 175 messages to the balloons, released them—and nothing happened. They were so weighted down they couldn't rise!"

A few balloons finally ascended, a message did come down close to the meeting place, and the helium holocaust was over.

Also during the summer of 1965 The Army was awarded a government grant to initiate the first Headstart program in Puerto Rico. Hepburn considered it an important step, with more than 100 children enrolled in the pre-school program. Though there were some complications and conflicts regarding the praying before meals, Hepburn felt that the adventure was worthwhile and with modifications it might have proved very successful a second year. He did feel that a disproportionate amount of funds was allocated for professional assistance as compared to that given programming.

Through the Headstart program and the academy, a community health program, which included visiting nurse services, was begun in the academy facility.

Outstanding assistance was given at this time to the Hepburns by the Caparra Terrace Home League, the first Home League on the island to achieve the coveted Standard of Achievement award. A number of Home League members accompanied Daisy on regular visits to beggars' homes, the leper colony, hospitals and prisons. "Several hospitals were our special interest," states Daisy, "and we joyfully became friends with the nuns who were responsible for the nursing care in one hospital for the chronically ill. The veterans hospital was not far from the corps and we visited there often. In each ward we were permitted to have a 20-minute service. We'd take our large visualized hymns and sing, and bring fruit and favors and enjoy this time with our servicemen."

Gifts for the needy from mainland groups were much appreciated and were often channeled through the Home League to recipients. For example, just before one Christmas, the Girl Guards of an Ohio troop sent 100 filled Christmas stockings. "What a time we had sharing these," Daisy remembers. "Another time we had a mothers' night party and were able to get cosmetic kits from the New York headquarters. The women were thrilled." Clothing boxes from the mainland were especially appreciated in the home for beggars, which had 75 residents. Here, regularly, the Hepburns conducted a service, then distributed whatever else they could, hopefully some fresh fruit, cookies and Kool Aid ("I've never made so much in my life!"), served with pretty napkins and mementos. The emaciated little men and women crowded round and smilingly accepted whatever clothes were passed out, even one time to Daisy's horror, several pairs of trousers with waistlines marked 38-SAMUEL HEPBURN. "Some of these dear little men would be lost in one leg," Daisy comments, "but it was the spirit that prompted the gift that is important, don't you think?"

Home League dinners as sources of income and events of good fellowship were frequent and always successful. Again, laughter and love transformed many occasions which might otherwise have proved disastrous. For example, consider the First Annual Caparra Terrace Lasagna Dinner—this was accomplished during the time the second floor was being added to the building; thus, there were no cooking facilities. Home Leaguers prepared the recipe "in everything from old broiler pans to cake tins." The food was then cooked in those homes which had ovens. 122 people who had bought tickets assembled under the evening stars on the patio, about to begin their first course of green salad which had already been placed on the table in individual, bright green salad bowls lent from a local hotel. Grace had been said, forks were lifted, then the rains came. Guests and cooks huddled under the garage carport—unsuccessfully. When the rains stopped all cheerfully helped empty salad bowls and fill lasagna platters. "The Lord gives and the Lord takes away. Blessed be the name of the Lord!"

Important to the Home League because of her infectious, spirit-filled contribution at a united Home League meeting, is Sally Olsen, Norwegian by birth and missionary extraordinary, a well-known and beloved person on the island. Called the Angel of the Prisons, for more than 10 years she had ministered to the material and spiritual needs of prisoners and had also founded a home for children. She told a remarkable story, one made more enchanting to Salvationists present by her testimony:

"When I was just a tiny girl, six years old, and living in my mountain village home, I gave my heart and life to Jesus when a visiting Salvation Army captain began to sing so beautifully:

'Teach me how to love Thee; teach me how to pray;
Teach me how to serve Thee better day by day.' "

The first Puerto Rican youth councils were conducted in 1965, held at a YMCA camp on the side of El Yunque Mountain, with Major Robert McNally, from the Eastern Territorial Youth Department, and Mrs. McNally, participating. Attending were young people from San Juan Temple, Caparra Terrace and Ponce corps.

A complete television program was produced in 1965, under the direction of Lieutenant Enrique Lalut, a blithe and energetic Chilean who had recently been trained for officership in New York and was now assisting with the Caparra Terrace corps and school program. Lalut, who captivated mainlanders by his delightfully original manner of speaking English, was shrewd and purposeful. He believes in the joy of salvation and in daring to accomplish whatever seems most likely to glorify God. He believes also in the efficacy of mass media. Here is his reminiscence on the subject:

"In my mind one of the finest ways in which we initially reached the public, let them know of our aims and capabilities, was through television and radio. The media people were kind and helped us to broadcast a 13-week program on radio. These were made through the kindness of the Mennonites, in their studios. Technically, these programs were not too professional, but they did great good. We received much comment, many letters from people hearing the gospel from The Salvation Army.

"One of the most helpful assistances on mass media was the television program on which we appeared with Jose Miguel Agrelot, a most marvelous and beloved Puerto Rican entertainer who has his own show, and plays the character, Don Cholito. We came to the show with a small group of officers who played brass instruments. Don Cholito was so happy. He put on a Salvation Army cap and played trombone along with us. That really went over big because he is so much loved, and we had such a good laughing time. We enjoyed ourselves. I can still see Majors Castillo and Smith playing with Don Cholito. That is when so many of the average people got to know The Army. They loved Don so much. He also made an interview with Captain Pagan, a very good one, and we got results. Always after, people were saying on the street, 'I saw you on television!' I see that program as the point from which The Army was really recognized, known for what it means, what it wants to be and do."

In 1964 Captain Hepburn taught and directed the first brass band in Puerto Rico, aided by the generosity of Lt.-Col. Paul Seiler, Sr., who has as one of his many hobbies the restoring of old instruments for use by overseas Salvationists. During the first graduation at Academia William Booth in May of 1964, 12 youthful academy bandsmen played two marches.

By 1965 the school had again grown to capacity. Teachers were now fully qualified and had teaching certificates.

General Frederick Coutts paid a short visit to Puerto Rico in 1966, meeting with the San Juan Advisory Board and addressing a large congregation; representing the people was the Secretary of State, Dr. Carlos J. Lastra.

The first island Salvationist wedding was conducted by Captain Roberto Pagan in 1965 when his sister, Milagros, married Hector Mendez, a teacher in the Academy and Salvationist who had trained at the Chicago School for Officers' Training.

In 1967 The Salvation Army participated in the crusade of Evangelist Billy Graham, Hepburn serving as publicity chairman.

By 1967 the student population of the academy was 110, children being served from kindergarten through sixth grade. Income from tuitions was increased from $5,700 to $13,000 between 1963 and 1967. The staff now included a full-time teacher for each class, plus a special English and music teacher, the school operated its own lunchroom and busing program. Captain Hepburn believed that by 1970 the school would have a population of 220 and Caparra Terrace would be self-supporting in both school and corps programs.

For the academy's fifth anniversary program, crowds of parents, relatives and friends overflowed the patio to share in praising God. One feature of the celebration was a parade through the Caparra area, for which police stopped traffic as the entire school body marched behind the Pentecostal church band. Highlighting the parade was the Valentine queen, who was resplendent in white satin—a dress made by her mother.

During 1966 Hepburn made a proposal to Territorial Headquarters for the Caparra Terrace operation which stated that the two programs (corps and school) should be separated in facility and budget to provide opportunity for each program to develop fully. He based his conclusion on the fact that the program, in his estimation, was more than one set of officers could effectively administer and that the facilities could no longer be effectively shared. Each was impeding the progress of the other.

He further noted that during his tenure the size of the student body had increased only 25 per cent though the cost per student had increased more than 100 per cent. The chief reason for inadequate enrollment, he believed, was that students moved to other schools after their fifth year to assure entry into the seventh grade. He believed that to have facilities available for complete day and evening programs, including music classes and adult night classes, would greatly ease the financial burden and help meet a grave Puerto Rican education need. He further felt The Army should enter the junior high program and later the senior high.

Concerning the corps program, he proposed that there be a full traditional corps program, a pre-school daily class, and that outreach be extended (it had already been started) into housing projects and slum areas.

In May, 1975, having just finished a research paper on educational problems in Puerto Rico for the University of Minnesota, Hepburn reiterated his belief in the 1966 proposal, and in the pressing need for higher education standards in Puerto Rico.

Heartbreaking to the Hepburns, during 1967 an administrative decision was made to close both the Caparra Terrace academy and another which had opened on September 3, 1963 in Ponce. At this time the two schools were absorbing an estimated 80 per cent of the annual budget, most of which was allocated from Eastern Territorial Headquarters. After study and consultation with the San Juan Advisory Board, Territorial Headquarters came to the decision that the schools were not financially viable and must be closed in favor of the needed establishment of Salvation Army social welfare services, to be initiated with the opening of Hope House. This multiplex welfare center included family service, transient service and lodging for men, which included two thrift stores and was supported by the collection of clothing and furniture.

Hope House was dedicated to the "glory of God and the service of mankind" in August, 1967, by Major and Mrs. Arnold Castillo, regional commanders. Special guest for the occasion was Mayoress Dona Felisa Rincon de Gautier who, in her remarks stated: "I am delighted to have The Salvation Army in Luna Street (notorious for crime and dissolution), where no one but The Salvation Army wants to work with my people." Later, she told another audience: "Indeed, Luna Street has much improved because of The Salvation Army."

Shortly after all of this took place the Hepburns were transferred to the mainland. Daisy Hepburn remembers the appointment as "four of the most remarkable years of our ministry," four years in which God gave them great blessing and opportunity. "We definitely left a good part of our hearts there. It was an opportunity that has been unequalled in our ministry. Never have we been in a place where our efforts to proclaim Christ were as readily or as open-heartedly received, and we thank God for the chance to have served."

Illustrative of the Power that keeps The Army marching in Puerto Rico and elsewhere despite disappointments and the ever-pressing need for personnel and finance, is the following story:

During the final year of their appointment in Puerto Rico, David received a phone call from a young woman soldier who, with her husband and children had been soldiers for some time. They had been won to God during street ministry in a nearby housing area.

"Captain! Captain!" the woman wept, "will you come and get Raphael out of the road? He's crouched in the middle, picking up little pebbles and pieces of glass and won't come in!"

David hurried to the home and found his friend and comrade seriously ill. Daisy took Maria and their two small children home with her, and David sought assistance. The Hepburns worked with the family until Raphael would not allow them or anyone else to visit, nor would he allow Maria to attend services. In his delusion, he struggled to protect his beautiful wife. The day before the Hepburns left Puerto Rico, Daisy cried as she hung up clothes outside the carport. One reason was that she didn't want to leave, and the other was that, at the moment, she was overwhelmed with sorrow because she wouldn't see her friend Maria before she left as Maria had no idea they were leaving. As she sniffled, there was a knock on the grillwork at the end of the carport, and there stood Maria. The two young women embraced, supporting each other in the knowledge that God works wonders, though they never expected to see each other again this side of heaven.

In 1973 the Hepburns visited Puerto Rico as directors of an evangelistic youth team and sought Maria and Raphael. From a little government-built cement-block house out they came—Raphael in his Salvation Army uniform minus the insignia, though he had no idea there would be guests. When Daisy got Maria alone, she asked, "How are you? He is so ill."

"Fine, Mrs. Hepburn, fine," said Maria. "I am all right."

"But how are you down in your heart? How have you been able to do it?"

Maria smiled peacefully. "It's the Lord. It's just the Lord."

Though still secluded, she was quite all right. And the couple's two children were growing up capable and sweet because, in Daisy's words, "She had found Christ and put Him to the test. In her way, she knew real victory."

> Why should life a weary journey seem?
> Jesus is my light and song.
> Why should I my cross a burden deem?
> Jesus is my light and song.
> All the way is marked by love divine.
> Round my path the rays of glory shine;
> Christ Himself companion is of mine.
> Jesus is my light and song.
>
> —EMMA JOHNSON

The Hepburns were succeeded by Captain and Mrs. Frank Payton, assisted by Lieutenant Brenda Leland. With the school closing, the Paytons found themselves with a large facility and a larger gap in the Army's work. "We organized a youth center in conjunction with the corps activities," recalls Payton. "The academy building was available, and we thought it best to do something for Puerto Rican youths. We changed the building a little and developed an after-school program."

PONCE

> *We are marching on with shield and banner bright,*
> *We will work for God and battle for the right;*
> *We will praise His name, rejoicing in His might,*
> *And we'll work till Jesus calls.*
>
> —FANNY CROSBY

On October 1, 1962, The Salvation Army opened fire in beautiful Ponce, second largest city in Puerto Rico, situated on the southern coast of the island, and facing the Caribbean Sea. Here, the climate is warmer and dryer than in San Juan, which is only 15-20 minutes flying time away, three hours by auto—over mountain roads which reveal verdant beauty of untrammeled forests and fields.

Directed by Captain and Mrs. Richard Shaffstall, the work was begun as an attempt to help homeless men by providing a hotel accommodation. The Shaffstalls were assisted by Mr. and Mrs. Henry White, former missionaries to China and Albania. Though need for the hotel soon proved insubstantial, many of Shaffstall's efforts became a strong foundation for the thriving work that exists today. Among his ventures was a shoe and clothing program which enabled 400 needy children a month to be enrolled in public schools. Shaffstall had made contact with a shoe company for the contribution of "seconds," and personally distributed them to three school areas.

He was appointed chaplain to the girls' reformatory outside Ponce—the first Protestant so appointed, and was instrumental in providing a school library. Gradually these efforts led to a working knowledge of corrections needed on the island. At one time The Army was invited to direct an orphanage through his contacts. During the Shaffstalls' first Christmas in Ponce, 3,000 persons were given food and on Three Kings Day, 450 children given toys. In addition, 500 persons were visited by the Shaffstalls in a yuletime League of Mercy program.

During regular visitation to the needy areas of Ponce, Shaffstall provided practical medical aid: he procured a mattress for an invalid found sleeping on the floor, a kerosene burner stove for a family who'd been cooking on an open fire; built a little home for an elderly lady; provided wheelchairs, got a sewing machine for a woman who would not go on welfare and said she could support herself and a daughter with the machine, which she did. "Most of this work is developing into a self-help project that will lift the living at a very nominal cost for several hundred persons in the area," reported Shaffstall at this time.

The initial spiritual ministry was largely an open-air effort, with the Shaffstall children passing out tracts and gospels while their parents preached, sang and prayed.

Shaffstall urged superiors to allow him to open a school, having explored education needs in the city, and was allowed to begin classes on September 3, 1963. The *Ponce Historical Record* of 1962 observed that "the Captain is filled with enthusiasm and has great hopes of raising a corps (member organization) right here in Ponce. The work was begun in a house, the school having nine members."

Shaffstall had observed a lack of proper English being taught in the schools. He started the school with Christian teachers who knew no Spanish, with a Spanish teacher who knew little English and then kept registration to 50 per cent Spanish- and 50 per cent English-speaking students. All instruction was in English except for a Spanish class and half the school chorus rehearsals. There was soon a waiting list twice as large as the enrollment. Shaffstall recalls, "There was perfect attendance and behavior at school. Teacher participation was excellent, and we enjoyed a very rewarding spiritual harvest as whole families were won to the Lord."

When the school was sold in 1967 because Salvation Army administrators believed it was not financially viable, there were officers who protested, strongly believing that the elimination of the school was a grave error. Now called the Caribbean School, the academy, under other auspices, is still the only English-speaking elementary and secondary school in Ponce and serves hundreds of children.

Within a few months of opening the hotel in 1962, as instructed, Shaffstall urged headquarters to close it. "I am convinced there is no need for a hotel for men here. The facility is in bad condition and the service isn't really needed." He was anxious to relocate the corps out of the hotel and felt there was a most pressing need for a corps-community center, noting that "In Ponce and at the University of Puerto Rico in San Juan the heads of the departments of social work have definitely expressed interest in such a place to use as a training ground for students majoring in social casework and physical education."

He recommended that The Army begin now to do something about a center which would house a gym, and that could double (by divider wall) as a drop-in lounge and a meeting-room for a golden-age club program, plus the usual office, rest rooms, game room and study room. "This could be built adjacent to, or separate from the site we would eventually be locating for school and corps and could include living quarters built with it."

He added that "the personnel to assist in the golden-age

program and community center program would be provided at no cost to us, courtesy of the government and the university. It would seem practical to approach several foundations to request a donation for the construction of the community center that would be interested in boys work."

In retrospect, Shaffstall regrets the loss of the boys' orphanage, plus the financial loss sustained when The Army had to buy the present property in Ponce and pay for the buildings "it could have had free."

The Shaffstalls were transferred to the mainland in 1964 and were succeeded in the command of Ponce by Major and Mrs. Frank Payton, who had two small children and a baby daughter born a month prior to their arrival. When they arrived, the Academia William Booth had been in operation for one year with a registration of approximately 100, and a Sunday meeting in English was being conducted regularly for day-school teachers. The majority of the students were children of employees of American corporations, mainly oil refineries and associated industries, although some were Puerto Rican children whose parents wanted them to learn English. The parents were eager to assist in any way possible.

Payton found recruitment of English-speaking teachers and the locating of a suitable school facility his chief problems. The academy had been located in a rented house to which Shaffstall had added a plywood kindergarten room in the backyard. It had served kindergarteners through fifth grade; however, previous to the Paytons' arrival, children had been registered for 7th and 8th grade so additional room was necessary. No suitable building could be found before opening day so temporarily the education building of the nondenominational United Church was used for kindergarten, first and second grades. This facility was on one side of town and the house, where the remainder of the grades were taught, was on the other. The rooms in the house were small and the children crowded.

It wasn't too long before a better school home was found through the interested inquiry of parents of some of the children, a large old house at Hostos Avenue 65, the vacated home of a contractor who now lived in Florida. Payton told the excited children to take their books and other learning materials home on Friday. "On Saturday," he recalls, "we had a great group of children and parents gather with us and, using a borrowed truck, moved the academy, lock, stock and barrel, into the new home, which had four classrooms. In addition, we built a classroom downstairs underneath the building, which was on cement columns, and one on the L-shaped porch." The school was conducted in English except for the Spanish class. Payton was unable to hire a first and second grade teacher, so Yvonne Payton taught that year. All classes accommodated two grades except for the kindergarten which was taught under the building.

During September of 1964, Captain Gilberta Hess arrived to assist in the work, having just returned to the island from a sick furlough. She was elated with her new appointment. "A fantastic experience," she recalls. "It was especially exciting because we were doing something new. When I got to Ponce, classes were being conducted in a little house and everybody was so crowded and so uncomfortable that when we finally moved to a bigger building everyone was thrilled even though the place seemed to be collapsing beneath us. It was my privilege to teach music to kindergarteners, first and second and fifth and sixth graders."

Most of all, Gilberta enjoyed Friday chapel service. "The students for the most part were children with whom I thought I should never work—American children whose parents had just about everything but who knew little about our Lord Jesus. They were so eager we started a Junior Legion for them. How captivated and captivating they were as they learned how to march forward as little soldiers of Christ's love."

During September of 1964, the Salvationists and two helpers, a teacher and their janitor, began to conduct open-air meetings in two of the housing project areas where they thought they could attract children and adults to meetings. Each Sunday afternoon they visited. "Captain Hess would have her accordion, and we would take all manner of flannelgraph lessons and visualized choruses," recalls Payton. "For several weeks we confined our children's efforts to these informal meetings, although we did conduct Junior Legion for the school children. Dozens of children would follow from one project to the other."

Immediately after the academy was moved to the house on Hostos Avenue, Payton announced to his street congregation that the academy bus would pick up any children who wanted to come to Sunday school the following Sunday. "We were packed out!" Captain Hess recalled later. "We didn't have enough room to put them. We didn't have enough teachers to teach them. It was a wonderful experience." About 60 children attended that first Sunday school.

At Christmas the Paytons wrote home: "There are many needy people here, in need of both spiritual and material help... our corps still has no permanent home but our hopes are bright for acquiring one soon so that the full potential of Salvation Army service to the community can be fulfilled."

The next activity to be started was a Sunday evening service. At first this was not too successful, and was for the most part attended almost exclusively by older young people. Also, about this time the Paytons began to produce a newsletter in Spanish which helped indoctrinate adherents, explaining Salvation Army terms, procedures and discipline.

Then came Home League. Although the Paytons were exceedingly busy with the academy, together with Captain Hess they started a Home League. "We depended a great deal on Gilberta Hess," states Payton, "for Sunday school and Home League." And Gilberta remembers it as the best Home League she'd encountered. "The ladies wanted to come; they enjoyed doing things, always excited about doing something new." The three shared not only the preaching and leadership of meetings but also heartaches and happiness as the corps of Ponce became a competent fighting force by the conclusion of 1964.

Torchbearers and Junior Soldier meetings were added soon after, although, Payton comments, "we didn't attempt to start everything at once but added activities as we felt we could manage them. Little by little the corps began to grow and we felt more and more a part of God's marching Army."

In June of 1965 Captain Hess was appointed to command the corps in San Jose, an outpost which was just being officially opened as a corps. Great difficulty was encountered in hiring qualified school teachers and Yvonne continued teaching the first grade for another year. Frank also did some English teaching, in order to help unburden teachers whose students were overly troubled with the language.

During the second summer, for one month the Paytons had enthusiastic help of Cadet Enrique Lalut, assigned for summer training from the New York School for Officers' Training; services were conducted in the main plaza, and an evangelistic campaign was conducted by Cadet Lalut and Fidel Gonzales, a soldier of the Caparra Temple corps.

The Ponce Advisory Board was formed in 1965, the majority of the members being parents of the school children, representing both Puerto Rican and American communities. One of its first projects was the sponsorship of an Easter visit from the Hempstead, New York, Salvation Army Youth Band which had been invited to the island by the Regional Commander, Brigadier W. Eldred Churchill. The municipal auditorium was secured and for an evening concert the board arranged with private and public schools for an historic event in the city's band shell to which 1,500 students marched from Ponce's main plaza.

The Paytons' third year was their most difficult one for they were without an assistant and Yvonne still had to teach. "There was jusy too much for two people to do," reported Payton. But, freed of teaching during the fourth year, Yvonne was able to give more time to supervision of the Home League, including in her programming a Home League contest. Women not only attended but also became eager to assist in visitation of the distressed and to participate in other corps and school activities.

As the corps grew, housing problems increased. Operating the corps program in the same facility as the academy was difficult and frustrating. Consider just the matter of congregational seating. As there was no assembly room, chairs from the schoolrooms had to be continually shifted—carried to the porch for corps services, to a spot underneath the house for chapel services. Up and down, in and out... in and out, up and down... a continual procession.

In 1967 Lieutenant Brenda Leland arrived to assist and delight the Paytons. Trained in the New York School for Officers' Training and bride-to-be of Lieutenant Enrique Lalut, she was a vivacious, talented young woman who, having dedicated her life to Spanish-speaking work, now was of immense help, keeping the books as well as assisting in both corps and school.

The major concern of the Ponce Advisory Board was still the

procurement of a proper school building, for unless the enrollment could be enlarged, Payton believed, financial solvency seemed improbable. The average enrollment was 110 and expenses were high. No adequate facility could be found, and Payton began to think that maybe it wasn't God's will to continue school operation. He had just read David Wilkerson's book, *The Cross and the Switchblade,* and had been much interested in the fact that Wilkerson had on several occasions "put out the fleece" requesting divine direction. He prayed, "Lord, if we don't have good indication of a piece of property by the end of 1966 I shall take this as an indication that You want us to stop with the school and go in another direction."

On the first of January, 1967, still with no school property in sight, he wrote a letter to San Juan headquarters requesting permission to fly to New York in order to recommend to territorial leaders that The Salvation Army change its goals in Ponce and close the school, especially since it was English-speaking and the corps work Spanish, although in Payton's words, "there was a good opportunity to preach the Gospel to the students."

Permission was granted. Strangely enough, two or three days before Payton left for New York, an ideal spot near the center of the city was found in which to establish a comprehensive Salvation Army corps-community program. Because this did not appear until a month after the date set for finding a school property, Payton believed that God desired to discontinue school work. The property was ultimately purchased, and Payton was able to do the planning and paper work before he left Ponce. In June the school was closed, also the academy in Caparra Terrace, Rio Piedras.

A few months later, Payton was appointed to attend a Spanish-speaking session at the International College for Officers, in London, and on his return to the island he with his family was to proceed to Rio Piedras to take command of the Caparra Terrace corps (now designated Caparra Temple). Also, Lieutenant Leland was assigned to help operate the first Salvation Army encampment for children and youths in Puerto Rico and in the autumn to proceed to Caparra Temple corps to again assist. When the Paytons farewelled, Captain and Mrs. Roberto Pagan, formerly corps commanders of the San Juan Temple corps, were appointed to replace them. With no school responsibilities, they were able to put full energies into building a traditional corps community center program. The big house on Hostos Avenue could no longer accommodate Army activities so, with the assistance of Fernando Colon, chairman of the Ponce Advisory Board, a new location was rented at 486 Street 8 in Constancia where the carport was turned into a sanctuary, and the Salvation Army program grew rapidly, so rapidly that the Pagans soon again found their work gasping for breathing space. The plot of ground Captain Payton had believed ideal was purchased and arrangements were made with a professional fund raiser to conduct a capital campaign to raise money for the construction of the Ponce Temple corps-community center and officers' quarters.

Though the campaign was a distressing failure, the USA Eastern Territory provided the necessary capital funds, and on February 14, 1971, a modern building with facilities for worship, Sunday school, office, kitchen and youth program, was dedicated to "the glory of God and the service of mankind" by Commissioner Paul J. Carlson and Major Arnold Castillo, then Regional Commander. From then on The Salvation Army in Ponce marched forward vigorously, led by the redoubtable Pagans until December, 1972—welcomed by the local citizenry, ministering to the poor and downtrodden, the young and defenseless, and ever calling to its ranks competent, dedicated soldiers, determined to:

> Make the world with music ring,
> While with heart and hand we sing
> Praises to our God and King, Hallelujah!

—CHARLES COLLER

LA PERLA

> "Whosoever heareth," shout, shout the sound,
> Send the blessed tidings all the world around,
> Spread the joyful news wherever man is found;
> "Whosoever will" may come.

—PHILIP P. BLISS

During the summer of 1965 Cadet Enrique Lalut[3] was appointed to Puerto Rico for summer assignment, and included in his ministry a daily vacation Bible School at San Juan Temple corps, with many children from nearby La Perla attending. Mrs. Brigadier Churchill wanted to start Home League meetings with the women of La Perla and it was arranged that the wife of the San Juan Temple corps commander, Mrs. Captain Roberto Pagan, would conduct these meetings in Spanish, assisted by Mrs. Churchill. The Cadet went along to corral the children. "Wherever he went, droves of children followed," remembers Mrs. Churchill. This was Enrique's introduction to La Perla.

Both the Smiths and the Paytons had helped the people of La Perla but no direct localized effort had been established. After Lalut's completion of his officer training he was reassigned to Puerto Rico, this time to assist the Hepburns at Caparra Terrace, but accepted responsibility for any Salvation Army duty that presented itself. He and Brenda Leland were the first Salvation Army officers to be married in Puerto Rico. Here is his characteristic observation of that occasion:

"We got married in a big Pentecostal church close to the Caparra Temple corps. That was when Major and Mrs. Castillo were Regional Commanders. Oh, it was a good time. We went in the afternoon, my best man, Captain Samuel Eliasen and I, to fix the steps that go to the altar. I guess we didn't do such a good job because Brenda almost fell flat on her face in front of all those people. A good time!"

Increased interest in the people of La Perla resulted in their becoming more interested, and, during 1967, the municipality asked The Army, with other agencies, to help alleviate existing distress by beginning a multifaceted program. Enrique and Brenda Lalut, then assisting at the Caparra Temple corps, were appointed to cooperate in the "San Juan Slum Project."

In La Perla, Enrique rented a basement room as a base for activities and began street and home visitation, and street meetings, to become acquainted with the people and their needs:

... Carmen was desperate. At 16 she needed $75 a day for drugs.

... Luis injected himself with six bags of heroin a day. Often in such circumstances small children were used to steal the necessary money. Would the Lieutenant go "cold turkey" with Luis?

... A very old man was found alone, ailing. "Go quick! Get the Lieutenant!" the people said. "He will know what to do—and do it."

... To stop serious infection health authorities decided that La Perlians needed four different vaccinations. But they didn't want *any.* Would the Lieutenant try to convince them? And they must have their eyes and blood and lungs and ears and teeth checked. Would Lieutenant arrange for them to help the people please? The Puerto Rican Medical Association was willing. The Job Corps was cooperative (their uniformed men helped keep order). Other specialists promised.

But the people didn't want help. The people didn't like all this fuss. The people wanted to be left alone. Enrique visited. Brenda visited. And visited and visited and visited. A final week of pamphlets and vivid description with a public address system brought the town to the nearby community center. The people needed medical aid, but they also needed furniture. The people needed clothing. But most of all the people needed somebody to cry when they cried, and laugh when they laughed. Enrique and Brenda proceeded to move in. Their quarters-hall was a tiny cottage among about 500 just like it. Now they were neighbors to the La Perlians.

"It was a good time Brenda and I had," comments Enrique. "We went to live there in the house now used for the corps. We used to have 70 kids going to the beach for Sunday school and for playing. It was very good. And this we couldn't have done without Felix. He was a lifeguard, loved kids and was good at any kind of sports. He became our Young People's Sergeant-Major."

The meeting of the two young men is interesting. Enrique was very tired during a weeknight meeting; only a handful of people were present and he was "wanting to get rid of the meeting." However, a troubled young man, Felix, had come in and wanted to come to the altar. He knew something of The Army because it had once befriended his family. "I didn't take him too serious," remembers Lalut, "but the Lord did a good job on him. He does a good job in spite of us sometimes." Felix got soundly converted and started to work with the children and teen-agers.

Later, Felix met Mildred and brought her to The Army. They were married, became faithful aides to the Laluts, helping in a variety of ways, among them conducting a most unusual Sunday school, with scholars being bused to the ocean, with the Bible lesson on the beach and a swim or a ballgame after. How many children? Who knows—sometimes 50, sometimes 100, sometimes more.

Soon, the children of La Perla belonged to the Laluts. Their parents were glad for a little more safety, a little more learning, a lot more love. Rafael is a good example: his mother was a prostitute and on drugs. "She used to," in Enrique's words, "go crazy sometimes, then she was taken to the hospital and poor little Rafael lived in the streets, sometimes for weeks." When the Laluts learned of this, they took Rafael home with them.

"Just helping like the rest do," Enrique tells you. "There is something about poor people. They are really nice to each other. You can drop into any house and right away they give you something to eat. If you are out of a bed, they give you a bed. You can sleep right on their sofa. There is something good of community feeling here. They are really nice among themselves. They really kind of step in and out of each other's houses and lives."

The Laluts wanted their adopted home clean and worked very hard with the nearby community center to make it so. "We tried to make our people conscious of cleaning up the place. Pigs, dogs, garbage everywhere. So we chose a day. Mayor Barcelo came to the quarters for tea. Then the paper took a picture of him and a garbage can and me." La Perla was clean for one week, but in Enrique's judgment, more time was needed to get the idea into the consciousness of the people, for La Perla was soon the same stewn and stricken community it had been.

Horse betting is popular in La Perla, and though people often don't have money for food, somehow 25 cents or a dollar is found for a bet. "That one guy was really making the money! He owned all the bars in La Perla. He didn't live there though. Once I went down to the shacks near the ocean. As I came to his house I stepped into it and here's this guy with $20,000 on the table. He ran a racing parlor for horses—filthy rich!"

Enrique had sometimes to deal with his people concerning betting. One soldier, "a nice girl," came into the testimony meeting praising the Lord because she'd just won $200 on a horse. "I had to give her hard doctrine, you know," states Lalut. "She also had more money because her nephew sold drugs. She didn't think it was wrong, and I had to take a lot of time to tell her that wasn't the right way of getting money."

The Laluts saw the hand of God in all. Once Brenda was alone in the little house when there was a heavy knock on the door. A man, "bleeding all over the place," stood there, gasping, "Where is the Captain? He's got to take me to the hospital! Quick! The Captain!"

The man had been in a fight a couple of houses down the street. "They almost killed the guy, you know," recounts Enrique. "But we got to know the people in their hearts this way. There were so many fights on that street. You know that's a center of drugs and prostitution in San Juan. Once, I remember in the middle of the night we were waked; we heard under us shooting guns and opened our door. This man found his wife with another man right there and started shooting at him. He was drunk and aiming not too good, because the guy left the house and ran down the street, this guy after him calling him names and shooting the gun. About 20 shots."

Preaching and praying opportunities abounded and were not without interruptions of many kinds. Once, Lalut recalls, he was preaching amid many people, with children sitting on top of the high wall (enclosing Old San Juan). "I wish I was like Paul altogether but I am not, for during that campaign I was preaching to all these people. A lotta kids listen. Then one fell down and broke his knee, so in the middle of the campaign I had to stop and pick him up and take him to the hospital. I wish I was like Paul so I could pray for him and he would be healed..."

The Laluts believe that anything can be done when it is for God and believers have sufficient faith. There is, of course, a secret. Says Lalut: "Our ministry in La Perla, besides the good it did to Brenda and me, showed that anything can be done when The Salvation Army wants to do it. Just this though: other churches had been trying to establish good work in La Perla for years. They worked hard too but couldn't establish that good work. But when we went down to live with the people we were part of the community. Then we could have people and a congregation. Then we could build the Kingdom on earth, you know that."

1st S.A. Building in Puerto Rico Dedicated

PONCE, P.R.—On the 10th anniversary of the opening of the work of The Salvation Army in Puerto Rico, Commissioner Paul J. Carlson, Eastern Territorial Commander, and a group of territorial leaders took part in the dedication of a new corps building, the first facility to be built by The Army of the island.

The Commissioner, who had been on the survey team which proposed the opening of the work here, said to the congregation, "Not only are we dedicating a building here today but we are also dedicating ourselves to service unlimited and undefiled."

Brigadier Lawrence Pickering, Regional Commander, introduced the Eastern Field Secretary, Colonel John Waldron, who chaired the program. Fernando Colon, Advisory Board Chairman, welcomed the crowd. Mayor Juan H. Cintron brought greetings and spoke of his relationship with Salvation Army service over the decade. The Rev. Donald Campbell of the ministerial association here said that The Army had discovered the secret of combining worship and service to mankind. Efrain Vassallo, Chairman of the capital campaign, assured the congregation that the best work is yet to be done.

The playing of the beginners' band under Markku Hamalainen won the applause of all. Pedro Mendez, architect and president of the Municipal Assembly, presented the keys to Captain Roberto Pagan, corps officer, who challenged his soldiers to service.

Also taking part were Lt.-Colonel Howard Chesham, Territorial Financial Secretary, and Major Stanley Ditmer, Territorial Youth Secretary. Captain Samuel Eliasen was translator.

The building consists of a 150-seat auditorium, an all-purpose room with folding doors for five classrooms, a nursery, home league room, kitchen and offices. Home Leagues of the Eastern Territory furnished kitchen counters, cupboards, a range and a refrigerator. The large parking lot will double as a playground.

Future plans include a basketball court and playground. Location of the corps is next to one of the neediest areas of the city. The building was made possible because of the concern and interest of the Central Finance Council, which made available a noninterest loan, pending the results of a capital campaign and other fund resources.

The five-day stay of the party from Territorial Headquarters included nine other events: a meeting with the staff and cadets of the extension School for Officers' Training; a reception at the Fortaleza by Governor Luis A. Ferre; a luncheon honoring Mrs. Comissioner Carlson given by the women's auxiliary at the Banker's Club in Hato Rey; divisional inspection; annual dinner meeting of the advisory board and women's auxiliary at the U.S. Naval Base at Miramar; officers' councils; holiness meeting at Ponce; salvation meeting at San Juan; and a united rally. Nine seekers were registered during the altar call at the rally.

The WAR CRY for May 22, 1971

550 Youngsters Enjoy Camp in Puerto Rico

SAN JUAN, P.R.—Some 550 boys and girls enjoyed one-week camping periods during a seven-week camp program run by The Salvation Army. Site of the regional camp is the Mennonite School in the central mountains of Puerto Rico several miles from town.

A special appeal netted $16,500 for the running of the camp. This included gifts of $500 from the telephone company, San Juan Rotary Club and Fundacion Fonalledas, Inc.

Mrs. Brigadier Lawrence K. Pickering, wife of the Regional Commander, was camp administrator. Captain and Mrs. Roberto Pagan and Lieutenants Victor Ortiz, Cesar Ferri and Fidel Gonzalez were program directors.

Louis Garner and Elvin Rodriguez, members of the Salvation Army Youth Service Organization of the Eastern Territory, were chief counselors and were responsible for some of the program.

Many seekers were registered at the chapel services held in the nearby Mennonite church. Following the camping program Carmen and Louis Davila, soldiers of the Caparra Temple Corps, began holding Sunday school on Sunday afternoon for campers from their neighborhood near Loiza, where The Army has not yet been able to open the work.

The superintendent of schools in Aibonito arranged for cooks and helpers of the school system to work at the camp without cost to The Salvation Army. Dr. G. Grayber and associates of the Mennonite Hospital in Aibonito gave their services.

The WAR CRY for August 28, 1971

Pittsburgh Youth Serves in Puerto Rico

PITTSBURGH, Pa.—Gayle Brindley of Dormont, daughter of Major and Mrs. David Brindley, flew to Puerto Rico with a team of Eastern Territory Salvation Army youths to be part of a "peace corps" type of program.

Four stateside members of the team will join with four Puerto Rican members to give joint impetus to improved Army service and personal contact in areas of need from June 21 to August 23.

Gayle, 17, is a 1971 honor graduate of Keystone Oaks High School and will be entering the freshman class of Indiana State University, Indiana, Pa., this fall. She is a member of the Pittsburgh Temple Corps and a cornetist in the band. She is also a soprano with a youth chorus, The Group.

This is the fourth consecutive summer in which a similar program has been sponsored in Puerto Rico by the Eastern Territory.

The WAR CRY for August 7, 1971

New Converts Won in San Juan Meetings

SAN JUAN, P.R.—Lt.-Colonel and Mrs. Moises Suarez of Hartford, Conn., conducted a 10-day campaign at the Temple Corps. Lieutenant and Mrs. Fidel Gonzalez, corps officers, reported several seekers, including eight new converts.

The dedication of an infant concluded with the parents giving themselves to the Lord. Mrs. Brigadier Lawrence K. Pickering, director of women's services, and the Home League participated in the women's night program. An open-air series, a Self-Denial altar service and officers' councils were features of the campaign.

... 72

The people of La Perla will tell you how they first began to believe in the walking, talking, working, loving, saving Jesus—when He moved in next door with the Laluts.

REGIONAL LEADERSHIP

Since The Army opened fire in Puerto Rico, it has been directed by seven Regional Commanders, a fact that does not augur for depth of understanding and continuity of effort; however, despite many reverses, the need for indigenous personnel, both lay and officer, increasing pressure for better facilities and programming; and need of money for both, The Salvation Army's march forward continues. Following is a list of Regional Commanders:

1961, September:	Sr.-Major and Mrs. Tobias Martinez
1963, January:	Brigadier and Mrs. Eldred Churchill
1965, September:	Major and Mrs. Paul D. Seiler
1966, August:	Major and Mrs. Arnold Castillo
1969, July:	Brigadier and Mrs. Lawrence Pickering
1972, January:	Major and Mrs. Ralph Leidy
1975, June:	Brigadier and Mrs. William Hazzard

The beginnings for the present Multiplex Welfare Center were effected by the second Regional Commander, Brigadier Churchill, when he picked up clothing and other articles in his personal car and stored them in a spare room at headquarters to be used for the needy (see Multiplex Welfare Center, Chapter III). The Army in Philadelphia, Pennsylvania, donated the first red truck in 1963. Mrs. Churchill was responsible for the opening of League of Mercy work.

The *War Cry* for June 29, 1963, carried this report from her: "We have started our first League of Mercy work, on a regional basis, here in Puerto Rico. Early in March our prospective Home League Secretary of San Juan Temple asked Mrs. Captain Bernard Smith and me to call on a friend, a missionary for 50 years. We found Miss Lydia Huber to be a charming woman who for many years has been interested in the children's T.B. hospital. She has been praying for someone to come who would be able to do more than she has been able to do. The Wednesday of Holy Week we visited the only hospital on the island, on the outskirts of San Juan, delighting 200 children with Easter eggs, scrapbooks and Bible Society booklets for older ones."

During Puerto Rico's centennial crusade, "Cristo para el Mundo," five visitation teams of 25 soldiers visited 3,000 San Juan homes; more than 1,000 residents attended evangelistic meetings. Eight new classrooms were added to the Army's Academia William Booth facility in San Juan, and Puerto Rican Salvationists received great inspiration from the General's one-day visit.

During January of 1965, the Eastern Territorial Financial Secretary, Lt. Colonel T. Herbert Martin, with Mrs. Martin made an official visit, reporting enthusiastically on the work, stating that he had attended a "United Home League rally" at Caparra Temple with 48 members present, inspected the school at Ponce, addressed the Junior Legion, inaugurated the San Juan Advisory Board, spoke to a fellowship breakfast group, brought the message at a holiness meeting at Caparra Temple, participated in open-air meetings at La Perla, addressed the annual meeting of the San Juan Advisory Board and strongly suggested "the possibility of an island-wide financial campaign," observing that nothing of this kind was being done by any welfare or charitable organization. "They do not exist in Puerto Rico."

He spoke of the pressing need for housing, bilingual officers and adequate funds, advising: "The Salvation Army should be patient... it only began three years ago, has no welfare institutions, and few people know what we are except those who have been in the States."

He then listed the following specific needs:
1. A home for unwed mothers
2. A welfare center from which family service and counseling can be done
3. A corps building for San Juan with school, chapel, recreation
4. A quarters for officers and assistants
5. A school or classroom for officer training
6. An old people's home

Of the Academia William Booth at Ponce he said: "The school is in operation... mostly for the children of Americans who work for Puerto Rican companies but prefer their children to go to American schools," concluding disappointedly, "One discouraging factor of the Advisory Board was the resignation of two bankers, due to local denominational influence."

There were many successful "firsts" now (see appendix for list) and occasionally there was an unsuccessful one; such was the projected opening of a corps in Mayaguez upon request from a citizens' group. Mayaguez, on the west coast, is the third largest city and third largest port on the island with a population of 90,000. Of it and other hoped-for openings, Churchill had commented to headquarters: "We feel that while we cannot open a new corps every month (Martinez's desire)... we see no reason why we could not do one a year without any increase in the cost of such an operation. In other words without increased deficit being borne by THQ...."

Soon, "the beautiful island" was under other leaders, Major and Mrs. Paul Seiler. The annual report for 1965 noted income of $156,991.70 from the following sources:

Donations and Christmas	8.7%
Program Earning, fees, specified gifts	44.6%
Eastern Territorial subsidy	46.7%

Expense: $157,075.40, distributed as follows:

Christmas and family welfare	4.6%
Central services	15.9%
School and corps	79.5%

Services rendered at this time included an emergency lodge, hospital visitation, seminars, institutes, rallies, retreat, emergency aid, Christmas welfare, Missing Persons department and counseling.

Known for his industry, innovative ability and foresight, Seiler felt the need for long-range planning and a clear view of major difficulties facing The Army in Puerto Rico. He prepared a report and proposal for Territorial Headquarters, including a plea that there be "more accurate understanding of needs at Territorial Headquarters," noting that the Puerto Rico Regional Commander "was not a directing executive authority but was operating only as a subordinate. Thus the problem of organization becomes the problem of building up between the executive at the center and the subdivisions of work on the periphery an effective network of communications and control."

He regretted that there was no brief of appointment other than that prepared by his predecessor, urging that a master plan was needed if more local support were anticipated (to insure successful local financing). "We do not have a program that merits public support to a greater degree than it is at present," he stated.

Regarding methods: "There are revolutionary changes taking place here at this very moment. There was a time when concepts of Salvation Army evangelism and related programs were universal at least in methodology, but I understand that even this has changed with the emergent crises in most countries in the world."

Personnel: "Personnel will continue to be a problem locally. Educationally qualified Puerto Rican people who have indicated a call to spiritual ministry feel they do not want to return to the island."

He believed that "first and foremost," Salvation Army leaders in Puerto Rico "must have the language of the people," that they at every level might become conversant with Salvation Army procedure. "We are not a church." A study of the cultural background was needed. Compassionate loving concern, a sincere desire to be of service—to win lost souls for Christ. Also, he strongly urged, "We must not labor under the false impression that Puerto Rico is like the Eastern Territory stateside appointments.

"At present the Corps Cadet program is grinding to a halt

because of reference books in English, inadequate translations of English into Spanish, lack of local leadership to teach. The music beat is different, and Salvation Army banding is a real challenge because of limited interest span.

"Location is important—we need to get out into the island. It is not imperative that we be downtown as long as we are within access of the city heart. Most people live out of the commercial centers. I do feel in Puerto Rico (outside San Juan) that all Salvation Army activities conducted in one community should be housed in the one compound. This would cut down on certain overhead items and allow a more complete use of facilities, equipment, personnel, etc."

The most urgent needs, Seiler believed, were:

1. Corps (including recreation and welfare facilities)
2. Community centers
3. Day nurseries
4. Training program for officer applicants
5. Camps
6. Occupational instruction centers
7. Girls' home and/or boys' home
8. Golden age center
9. Schools
10. Hospitals

Regarding finance: "We know that Puerto Rico will not be self-supporting for years to come. The program will, of necessity, have to be financed from external sources if it is to be continued or expanded. We are aware that a multi-faceted program receives greater support more quickly... budgets should be more realistic... every officer should be expected to make greater effort and seek ways to finance this work... I personally feel that a financing program must be set up to carry on the work in Puerto Rico. This should be done by Advisory Board representatives (San Juan and Ponce), Territorial Headquarters and two island officers.[4]

In August of 1966, Major and Mrs. Arnold Castillo succeeded the Seilers. These were Salvationists with long experience in Argentina, notably contributing in the translation of teaching and other materials for both youth and adults. Churchill, Seiler and Martin had stated this critical need before them.

In 1967, the first summer encampment for children was held at Aibonito and the Hope House welfare center was opened. Other "firsts" effected during the Castillos' tenure are:

> La Perla community project
> First Home League camp
> Thrift store on Buenaventura Street
> First summer camp
> First Christmas distribution of food bags (1966)
> Inauguration of Future Officers' Fellowship
> First FOF seminar
> First series of weekly radio programs

To give an indication of the growing work, in 1966, 351 families were assisted, with 2,266 persons involved in helping, and 5,359 toys distributed, with a welfare expenditure of $14,632.16. One thousand seven hundred and forty meetings were conducted, with an attendance of 39,381. Out of a budget of $307,223.10 the subsidy from Territorial Headquarters was $89,966.25. At that time, projected programs included a servicemen's club, day-care center, School for Officers' Training and the opening of the Mayaguez corps.

During the summers of 1968-69 Bandmaster David Appleby of the Manhattan Citadel New York corps, expertly directed the SAYSO youth group in Puerto Rico and St. Thomas campaigns, which lasted approximately two months each summer. The groups gave leadership and participatory service in manifold ways, including indoor and open-air meetings, Daily Vacation Bible schools, staff teaching in the island music camp, door-to-door visitation, Bible study groups, musical festivals, service club program, institutional visitation, radio and TV programs and clean-up, paint-up projects.

Major Bernard Smith, who accompanied the 1968 group on tour concluded his report to Territorial Headquarters: "Never (in this location) has so much been accomplished by so few in so short a time." Though the language barrier was burdensome, extreme and often permanent interest was shown by Puerto Rican listeners. Smith's report noted, ". . . many diligent inquiries were made by people in need of Christ," some life decisions being made later by persons first attracted to The Army and to God by SAYSO young people.

Brigadier and Mrs. Lawrence Pickering replaced the Castillos in July of 1969 and, shortly after, the Puerto Rico extension school of the New York School for Officers' Training was commenced, with Major Frank Payton administrating at the Caparra corps facility, assisted by island officers.

The first session was composed of six cadets, three couples, who were in charge of corps in San Juan. In addition to their corps command, they attended classes five mornings each week and participated in other phases of training. The undertaking resulted in the first New York commissioning of Lieutenants from Puerto Rico, with the Commonwealth's Secretary of Social Services, Ephraim Santiago, and the Army's Advisory Board Chairman and Mrs. Peter Martinez attending.

It was a stirring event as the Puerto Rican cadets marched in with the flag of their country and were commissioned with their mainland session mates. The next year's cadets were resident, with accommodations at Regional Headquarters, in Puerto Rico. Their second year of training was administered in New York. This program of training was later modified to give cadets two years at the School for Officers' Training in Suffern, New York, with a summer of field work.

Also during 1969 the Puerto Rico Women's Auxiliary of San Juan (for which Mrs. Major Castillo and Mrs. Major Bernard Smith had laid the groundwork) was inaugurated. Since that time it has become very active. Here is an excerpt from the official report:

"The Greater San Juan Women's Auxiliary of The Salvation Army was inaugurated and officers installed on November 7 by Lt.-Colonel Mrs. Emma Howarth of Territorial Headquarters, New York City, at a noon luncheon meeting at the Swiss Chalet Restaurant. The Auxiliary has been active for several months and has now become a registered unit of The Army, directed by Mrs. Brigadier Lawrence K. Pickering of the Puerto Rico regional office. Sixteen ladies comprise the charter members. Serving as Auxiliary officers: Mrs. Philip Neild, President; Mrs. Jaime Sitiriche, Vice-president; Mrs. Harry Carlisle, Treasurer; Mrs. Peter Martinez, Secretary; Mrs.

Weldon Manwaring, Public Relations. Auxiliary committees are: Youth Committee, Nominating, Membership, Fund Raising, Service Projects, Christmas, and Hope House."

The Auxiliary's first project was to raise money for 60 Sunbeam uniforms. In 1972-75 they sponsored fashion shows in conjunction with Sears Roebuck and Company to benefit The Army.

In January of 1972, when Major and Mrs. Ralph Leidy became Regional Commanders, there were four corps, plus a community center in La Perla; a welfare center; cadets' training program; and a summer camp. Major Leidy saw the need for The Army to conduct its own financial campaign, with the ultimate goal of $200,000, which would make the work free from subsidy. When he arrived, he states, there was a badly managed United Fund in San Juan which needed a name agency with appeal, known to American communities. They needed that name, and an independent campaign by The Salvation Army would hurt them. Yet, they couldn't afford an allocation of $200,000, so a compromise was worked out with an initial allocation of $50,000, with annual increases of $50,000.

In 1972 the La Perla center was made a corps, with Lieutenant Eric Diaz in command; Hope House was moved to an unused Salvation Army-owned building in Caparra Terrace (part of the early purchase) where Captain Cesar Ferri, the Regional Welfare Secretary, expanded the work to become a Men's Social Service program. At the resignation of the San Jose officers, the corps was closed, having been opened in 1965, and work was opened in Guayama.

The first regional Corps Cadet rally was held in 1973, organized and supervised by Mrs. Major Castillo, Youth Officer.

In January, 1974, a corps was opened in Loiza, a small community about 25 miles east of San Juan, with Lieutenant and Mrs. Victor Ortiz as commanding officers. In July of 1974 a corps was opened at Mayaguez with Sergeant and Mrs. Hernan Fourquet in charge, but was closed when Fourquet resigned and no other leadership available. The corps was reopened in 1976.

Also in 1976 a corps was opened at Caguas, with Lieutenant and Mrs. Eric Diaz in charge.

In July of 1973, Salvationists Douglas and Zaida Marti moved to the Bayamon area and, realizing the need for a worship center, started one in their carport. They had no money. "But the Lord provided everything we needed," they recall. "A lot of people gave us a little bit to prepare God's House." The Martis later became commanding officers of the Tremont Corps Community Center in the Bronx, New York.

Twenty-four persons attended the first Sunday morning service, and "the work marched on." They soon had a "beautiful Sunday school" with two classes and a mid-week Bible study service besides their Sunday adult meetings. "Soon we had to move to a larger home because our carport was too small," states Marti. "Members began picking up people in their cars, and so we grew and grew. Of course, we thought our growing congregation could only be The Salvation Army, so we started to give soldier classes and conduct open-air meetings." Again they outgrew their home and moved to a larger one. Soon they had commissioned nine Senior Soldiers and seven Junior Soldiers. A Home League was begun and, in their words, "the work just kept marching forward."

During 1975 the United States Virgin Islands were added to the Puerto Rico Command.

UNITED STATES VIRGIN ISLANDS

ST. CROIX, ST. JOHN, ST. THOMAS

God's trumpet is sounding,
"To arms!" is the call;
More warriors are wanted to help on the war,
My king's in the battle. He's calling for me!
A salvation soldier for Jesus I'll be.

On land and on water my colors I'll show
Through ten thousand battles with Jesus I'll go;
In danger I'm certain He'll take care of me,
His blood-and-fire soldier forever I'll be.

—FREDERICK BOOTH-TUCKER

ST. THOMAS

When in January of 1973 the Virgin Islands were transferred from the West Indies Territory of The Salvation Army to the USA Eastern Territory, directly responsible to the Puerto Rico regional office, the corps facility of the Charlotte-Amalie corps, the only one on St. Thomas island, was in tragic disrepair due to lack of funds, but the corps itself was intact, even aggressive, having survived many onslaughts since it was opened in 1917. Because of distance from other Salvation Army operations it had known little Army supervision, once having gone without an off-island visitor for 12 years. Nevertheless, Salvationists conducted regular services, including open-air meetings, helped the poor, visited the ill and imprisoned, preached and prayed and sang in true Salvation Army tradition.

During two periods, Major Iris Hawkins, an English missionary officer, commanded St. Thomas, with great dedication. She was assisted in the first appointment by Lieutenant Mai Marklen (now Mrs. Hodges), also Swedish, who resigned officership for island marriage and today, with her children, serves faithfully.

Official records of the opening and continual service of the Charlotte-Amalie corps are non-existent, but Albertina Scatliffe and Adjutant Agnes Baker remember these days very well. Albertina, who on July 5, 1975, was 82 years old, is an alert historian and has followed The Army since shortly after it was opened. Agnes Baker, now retired in Brooklyn, N.Y., was one of the first children converted and enrolled as a Junior Soldier and entered Salvation Army officership from the Charlotte-Amalie corps.

Agnes Baker first heard the Army drum beating "at my corner which was a stone's throw from my house." She looked out a window but didn't pay attention because only one oddly dressed man comprised the invading force. However, the next day The Salvation Army was the talk of the town. No one had ever heard of The Salvation Army, and the beating of its drum in the name of God caused great offence. Adjutant Trotman, that first dauntless officer, had come from Barbados with "God's cannonballs in his blood." The second day of the attack he distributed invitations to a religious service, horrifying St. Thomians who demonstrated their objections in a variety of unpleasant ways, some of them physical. Little Agnes was forbidden to attend meeting, but she was so noisily determined that eventually a curious adult accompanied her to a meeting where she felt called immediately to officership.

Agnes became a Junior Soldier, studied her Bible in a mood of fascination and soon was helping direct the company meeting (Sunday school). As soon as she was old enough she became a Corps Cadet, a leader of the Band of Love and a hospital visitor. And it wasn't too long before she realized her childhood calling, becoming a Salvation Army officer.

Unlike Agnes Baker, Albertina Scatliffe was not called to officership but remained a soldier in the Charlotte-Amalie corps throughout her life. She was invited to meetings by a daughter. For 15 years she attended before she "gave in and came to the mercy seat. Then I became a blood-and-fire soldier," she testifies. Though her husband was drowned in a fishing accident in 1926, and three of her four children are dead, the surviving daughter being blind, Albertina is a plucky, happy Salvationist whose chief delight is rhythmically whamming the bass drum in the open-air ring—a battle practice for more than 50 years. Also, gratis, for many years she has kept the hall clean and has washed and ironed the officers' white uniforms as a gift to God.

Adjutant Trotman was soon assisted by Cadets Lesprance and Tobin, both of British Guiana. "The spiritual work leaped!" recalls Adjutant Baker. "Souls got saved. Drunkards came. Many seekers became soldiers. They wanted to serve God more and more." However, such zeal brought bitter physical persecution, both from religious and secular sources. Salvationists were ridiculed and stoned. The words, "Floor rollers!" were screamed at them. Then one night an organized band of religious fanatics stormed into the hall and destroyed everything—but the Salvationists. "We simply marched on," says Agnes Baker.

The second location was given by a Mrs. Manneke, a black woman whose husband was white. A garage sheltered the town hearse on this plot but was soon converted into a first-class hall by Adjutant Trotman.

A change in command brought Adjutant R. Bishop, also a Barbadian, to St. Thomas as commanding officer. He was assisted by Lieutenant G. Holder of British Guiana; and Cadet Airall of Antigua.

Adjutant M. Phillips followed Adjutant Bishop in command of the corps. In 1922, the Charlotte-Amalie corps proudly offered two candidates as field cadets to fight for King Jesus in other lands: Eugenie Smith and Agnes Steele.

In pioneer days, the Army's best friends were among the business people. Merchants were generous in helping The Army serve the needy, and often gave both material and spiritual support. A storekeeper, Mrs. Parlack, was certainly a sustainer of the soldier-saints, in Adjutant Baker's memory.

Lay leaders who gave heroic service during the first five years include the following:

Corps Sergeant-Major Mercer
Corps Cadet Guardian Blyden
Flag Sergeant Fabio
Orderly Branch
Penitent-form Sergeant Mrs. Fabio
Young People's Sergeant-Major Smith
Brother and Sister Todd
Sister Fabio
Sister Branch

"God bless them all!" states Adjutant Agnes Baker. "I was there and I know!"

The first open-air meeting was held at Dover Street, and the first chorus sung was "Where Shall You Be When the Last Trumpet Sounds?" This amazing schedule of Sunday meetings gives some idea of the discipline required of the soldiers who participated in Salvation Army activities all day:

5 a.m.	Rise
10 a.m.	Open-air service
11 a.m.	Holiness meeting
3 p.m.	Company meeting (Sunday school)
4 p.m.	Open-air service
5 p.m.	Open-air service
7 p.m.	Salvation meeting

In 1919 or '20 the first dinner for the poor was managed with great prayer and industry, the merchants doing "splendidly." Doing splendidly often amid persistent hardship well characterizes the St. Thomas Charlotte-Amalie corps throughout the years.

The present property was given by Alfred Lochart, a local millionaire and under the direction of Captain Morris, the soldiers built the hall. This building, though small, is a remarkable structure, sturdy and inviting, with unglazed gothic windows and door, open to the ocean breezes except when shuttered at night and during storms. Major and Mrs. Mario Jourdan, while corps commanding officers, renovated the building, including the planting of bushes and flowers, the Major being an amazing "green thumber." Herein today are the usual paraphernalia of an Army hall: Sunday school register, Bibles, songbooks, decorative appointments contributed and arranged by the Home League, a small platform, pulpit and, of course, the beloved penitent-form.

About 18 years ago, Major Hawkins, aided by her soldiers, built a quarters attached to the meeting-hall in the rear. This space is now being used for classes and conferences. Major Hawkins continued in command until Major and Mrs. Jourdan replaced her in 1974.

When the Jourdans were appointed to regional headquarters in Puerto Rico, Commanding Sergeant and Mrs. Evan Thomas, lay leaders in St. Thomas, responded to the need for leadership and on October 2, 1974, were appointed to command the Charlotte-Amalie corps, with responsibility extending to St. Croix. Recently, about two dozen St. Thomas soldiers paid their own expenses to conduct an open-air campaign on the sibling island. Under the direction of Brigadier and Mrs. Hazzard, Regional Commanders, the first League of Mercy work was begun on St. Croix, including institutional visitation, worship services and dinners served to the needy at Christmastime. Service Unit work was begun after Hurricane Eloise in 1975, by Captain Samuel Eliasen. St. Croix residents were especially receptive after observing The Army at work following the hurricane. Led by Sister Doris Archibald, Home League Secretary, the St. Thomas Home League has a busy and effective ministry; and eager St. Thomas soldiers march to new engagements for God. For example, consider the Sunday school conducted for almost eight years on Sunday afternoons by Sister James, now assisted by Sisters

Archibald and Brooks. Sister James, middle-aged and portly, is no Sunday soldier. Her faith has been forged in many a furnace of affliction. Nothing precious has been lost, and her smile, her calm, and her effectiveness have been intensified.

Eight years ago, in the housing project where Sister James lives, she felt led to conduct a Sunday school for neglected children. The management of the project, however, refused to let her use the recreation room, fearing an abundance of requests. Sister James persevered, won and no one complained. What singing and hand-clapping, what learning and living followed! But through the years, with each change of management, Sister James had to ready her ammunition. She's had considerable experience, knows how to load a spiritual weapon and how to fire it. Which she does.

Having interviewed Sister James, we sneaked a peek during final prayer moments of a Sunday morning service—and were baffled to observe the saint sitting, eyes wide open, thumbing through her songbook. We watched. She did not close her eyes but continued to read. Occasionally she would whisper, "Thank you, Jesus," but her concentration was on that book.

After service, we couldn't restrain our curiosity.

"Sister James, what were you looking at in the songbook? We peeked."

"Oh," she said, with a smile as broad as her big black hand, "number 529. Isn't it wonderful!" Together we opened her songbook and read: "How wonderful it is to walk with God, along the road that holy men have trod. . . ."

"Wonderful, isn't it," said Sister James, "how it settles a person—walking with God."

Walking with God. No wonder the St. Thomas corps managed 12 years without a visitor. Their residential Leader was able. And is. Perhaps you too would like to see the song held in Sister James' heart for so long. Perhaps your soul will be settled too:

> *How wonderful it is to WALK with God,*
> *Along the road that holy men have trod;*
> *How wonderful it is to hear Him say:*
> *"Fear not, have faith, 'tis I who lead the way!"*

How wonderful it is to TALK with God,
When cares sweep o'er my spirit like a flood;
How wonderful it is to hear His voice,
For when He speaks the desert lands rejoice!

How wonderful it is to PRAISE my God,
Who comforts and protects me with His rod;
How wonderful to praise Him every hour,
My heart attuned to sing His wondrous power!

How wonderful it is to FIGHT for God,
And point poor sinners to the precious Blood;
How wonderful it is to wield His sword
'Gainst sin, the enemy of Christ, my Lord.

How wonderful 'twill be to LIVE with God,
When I have crossed death's deep and swelling flood!
How wonderful to see Him face to face,
When I have fought the fight and won the race!

—THEODORE H. KITCHING

ST. CROIX AND ST. JOHN

O boundless salvation, deep ocean of love;
O fullness of mercy Christ brought from above;
The whole world redeeming, so rich and so free,
Now flowing for all men come roll over me.

—WILLIAM BOOTH

Very little information is available concerning The Salvation Army on the island of St. Croix and none regarding St. John. It is known that a Salvation Army corps once existed on St. Croix, housed in a rented building in Christiansted. During the early 1950's, when there was no commanding officer, the owner of the property asked The Army to vacate the building. The aging Corps Secretary, Mrs. Geraldine Rouse, was determined to keep The Army marching and cherished both the Army flag and the drum in her home. Regularly she conducted corps meetings in the street, including Sunday school and open-air services.

Finally, due to age and illness, Secretary Rouse became incapable of such strenuous service but continued to *be* The Salvation Army, displaying both flag and drum in her home. From time to time, Salvationists from St. Thomas visited though travel expense was almost prohibitive. In June, 1959, a public meeting was held by The Salvation Army at which the present Corps Cadet Counselor, Mrs. Mai Hodges, was present. Held in the Pilgrim Holiness Church, the meeting was conducted by the Territorial Commander for the West Indies, Colonel John Stannard, with Dr. Melvin H. Evans, who later became the first elected Governor of the U.S. Virgin Islands (1970-74), bringing the message.

A later visit, in April, 1972, was paid to Mrs. Rouse by Major Shirley Cox, then commanding officer in St. Thomas, and Mrs. Hodges. Mai remembers, "When we greeted Secretary Rouse in her home, she was speechless with delight and thrilled with our plans for an open-air campaign by St. Thomas Salvationists. We agreed to return on Easter Saturday."

Before parting, the three decided to sing an Army song and simultaneously suggested, "O Boundless Salvation."[5] They opened their songbooks and began, but by the time the third stanza was reached, they were weeping too hard to continue. "We felt God's presence right there with us," recalls Mai. "Then each of us prayed that He would continue to bless The Salvation Army and sustain Secretary Rouse."

During the promised visit, Secretary Rouse was ecstatic, joining in with praises to her God. Wherever the group witnessed during the day, the same question was asked: "When is The Salvation Army coming to St. Croix? We need you over here."

Through the years, Secretary Rouse and Mai Hodges corresponded, with Sister Rouse continually testifying to her faith in the Lord Jesus and His glorious keeping power. She looked forward to hearing a Salvation Army band come marching down the street, the soldiers singing as they followed, but did not live to know that joy. In June of 1975, Secretary Geraldine Rouse was Promoted to Glory[6] — still a soldier of salvation, still victorious.

. . . 88

And still comes the question, "When is The Army coming to St. Croix? We need you here."

St. Croix will be re-invaded soon. Preparations for a comprehensive work have been begun, and during Christmas, 1975, regional staff members from Puerto Rico cheered many with gifts and a celebration service in the island hospital, hospital annex and a senior citizens' home, also providing a festive dinner for senior citizens. The embryo Service Unit helped plan the events and are eager that Salvation Army services and activities be commenced as quickly as possible.

Beachheads established!

Notes

1. Medarda Melendez is now retired and living in Orlando, Florida.

2. The Pagans are Puerto Rican. During the early 1960's while living in Chicago, Illinois, they were converted under the ministry of Raul Guerrero, a Chilean Salvationist tailor who singlehandedly started Chicago's Spanish-speaking work.

3. A young Chilean whose parents had spent many years as Salvation Army missionaries in Bolivia and Chile.

4. Excerpt from "Observations and Recommendations," Major Paul D. Seiler report, March, 1966.

5. Most beloved of all Salvation Army songs; composed by its Founder, William Booth.

6. Salvationist term for death.

PUERTO RICO

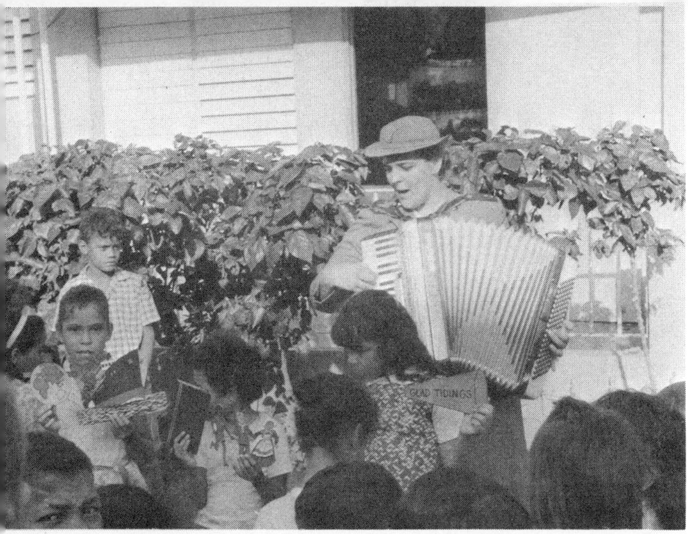
GLAD TIDINGS

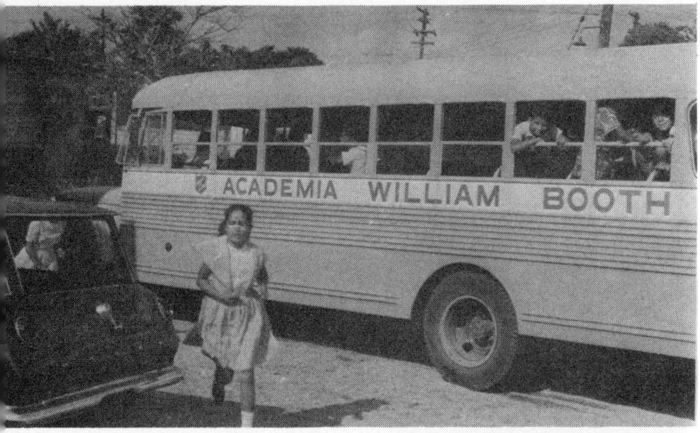
ACADEMIA WILLIAM BOOTH

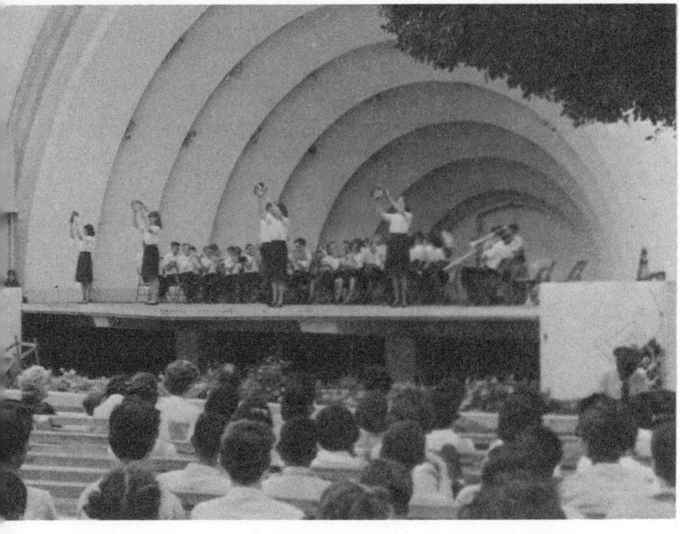

PUERTO RICO

VIRGIN ISLANDS

First soldiers of the St. Thomas corps, with officers (about 1920).

St. Thomas, Virgin Islands: Daniel Ambrose, Government Secretary, gives keys to the officer in charge, at the dedication of the corps building, 1940.

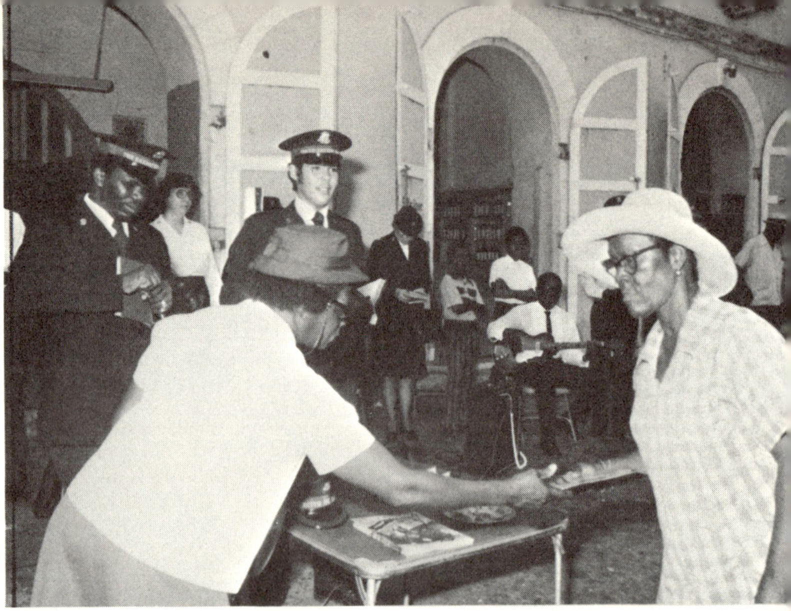

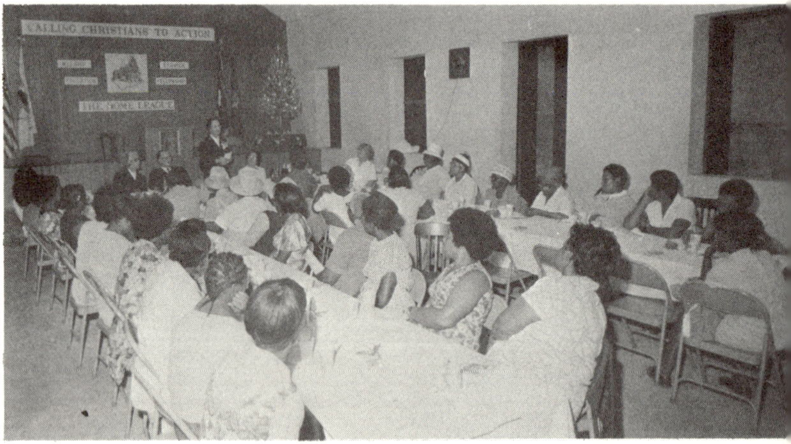
CALLING CHRISTIANS TO ACTION

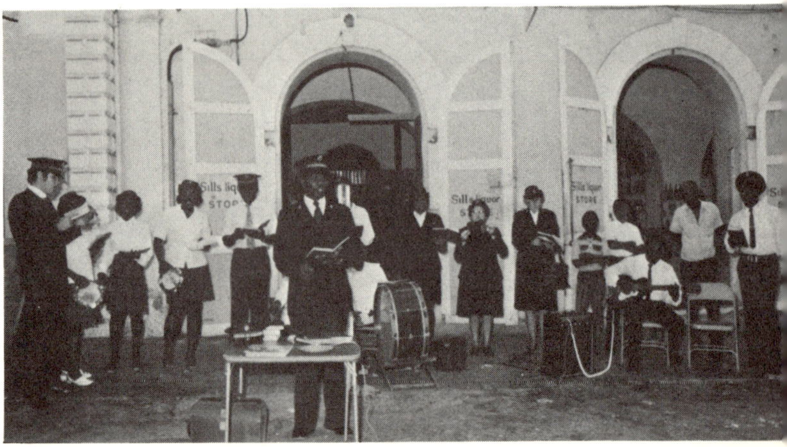

VIRGIN ISLANDS

On to the conflict, soldiers, for the right,
Arm you with the Spirit's sword and march to fight;
Truth be your watchword, sound the ringing cry:
　Victory, victory, victory!

　　Ever this the war cry,
　　　Victory, victory!
　　Ever this the war cry,
　　　Victory!
　　Write it on your banners,
　　　Waft it on the breeze,
　　Victory, victory, victory!

—WILLIAM HOWARD DOANE

CHAPTER III ───────────────────

Review Troops

Now to the present. In 1976 Salvation Army work includes Regional Headquarters, five corps-community centers, family welfare and Men's Social Service sections, summer encampment for children, correctional services, League of Mercy (for institutional and other visitation), program for runaway youths, Nurses' Fellowship, two Service Extension units (Caguas and Humacao, with projected openings in Arecibo, Cayey, Mayaguez and St. Croix), and the services of two Advisory Boards and a Women's Auxiliary. Whether or not, in remembering Her Honor Dona Felisa's admonition,[1] The Army has proved itself worthy of Commonwealth support and must be judged by the Puerto Rican people. It has been, has meant, something; certainly not enough, especially if expressed in terms of the diversified needs of so many groups and individuals, both hidden and imminently visible. Always present are the destitute citizens of Grandstand in Guayama, the proud people of Loiza's Mediania Alta barrio and La Perla, the blank stares and moans of aging prostitutes along the balconied calles of Old San Juan, and the upturned hands of street beggars.

During an interview with Ray Owen, a Salvation Army Advisory Board member in San Juan, we realized the proportions of the challenge. Owen, a mainlander and director of Radio Station WAPA, was asked the inevitable question:

"In its traditional role of loving God by helping man, what should The Salvation Army do that will most effectively help the Puerto Rican people?"

The lank Owen frowned.

"I don't know. All it does looks good to me. I go to visit the operations. I'm accepted because I'm with a Salvationist. . . . Wait." He pressed a button and Angelina Hernandez, his comely secretary, entered. "Angie, you grew up here. Sit down and answer this question. Don't hurry." He repeated the question. "Tell us what you think."

Angie took time to answer. This is what she said, her gentle gaze direct:

"The Salvation Army wishes to help my people?"

"Yes."

"Then The Salvation Army must be careful. We need much, but most of all we need to keep our pride. Don't give us charity. Don't degrade us."

"Our aim is to help man become self-responsible under God."

"Good," said Angie. "Then help us. But let us help you help us."

"How?"

"Let it be a cooperative effort. Let us give in return. Let us help build and maintain the buildings in which you serve us. Let us go with you to our bruised and hurt ones. Let us provide advice, then allow us to help follow that advice."

"How will this best be done by The Salvation Army?"

Angie allowed herself time.

"May I put the truth this way." She raised both slender hands, drawing attention to them. "The answer—for our people, our country, is only this: *one hand upon another.*"

She completed the gesture.

Later, I discovered that Angie is a salvation army in herself. Alone she visits hospitals, alone she cares for children, alone she takes the elderly for rides, alone she dreams bigger dreams of involvement. She had hoped once to become a social worker to help her people, but there were financial restrictions. Thinking of another problem she'd mentioned concerning need, we remembered her saying, "There is a particular difficulty. Often, the most deserving won't seek help."

Among thousands of hungry mouths, worn shoes, barren minds, aching hearts, ailing spirits, still help the child who brushes against you? The man who drunkenly swears at your uniform? The aging woman lying like withered lettuce by the curb on Calle Tetuan and Calle Sol calling to you for help?

Perhaps the successes of The Salvation Army thus far in Puerto Rico have been due to Angie's concept of one to one, and its failures have resulted from the lack of its application. It is a premise to be tested. The work has some solidarity and form; there is zeal and for the most part, good spirits, increasing visibility and the will to become self-supporting though the work is still heavily subsidized by the United States, which is regarded by some as the saintly Santa in blue. Especially interesting is the fact that many men—action-oriented, intelligent young men and older men with families—are becoming involved as volunteer workers, soldiers (lay members) and officers (ordained ministers).

Guayama resident Eduardo Rovira-Sanchez, a leading businessman who is knowledgeable concerning religious, education and economic needs of his people, was questioned regarding the Army's contemporary role in Puerto Rico.

"It is time for The Salvation Army to march across the island," he said. "It can do what no other church or organization can do. Recently, I was talking with priests of my city regarding The Army and they said, 'By all means do all you can to help The Army. We know it from the states, and Salvationists do only good. They reach the people we cannot.' "

Though The Salvation Army is non-partisan and officers may not make personal political views public, all effort nevertheless has political implications, so we asked, "How does The Army fit the political scene here?" We were told that both statehood and Commonwealth parties stand for self-responsibility of the individual, for freedom of religion and for retention of the identity of Puerto Rican citizens. "It means," said Mr. Rovira, "that only the revolutionary five per cent oppose your purpose and practice. If the people are led to God, they will not be overcome by plaints and promises of a few."

In summarizing educational needs of Puerto Rican applicants seeking to enter Salvation Army ranks as lay or officer leaders, we mentioned problems inherent in such desires. There is difficulty with English (as officers, they will need to speak English on the mainland), and general concern with the student role. Several methods of teaching have been tried with a summer of field work included in each: two years' teaching in Puerto Rico administered by Regional Headquarters and corps officers; a year's teaching in Puerto Rico with a year in the New York School for Officers' Training; and (as at present) two years in the New York school. Still, preparation does not seem adequate.

When asked for advice, Mr. Rovira said: "The difficulty is not in the lack of ease with the English language but in the substandard education which still prevails in Puerto Rico. You will not help by reinforcing the speaking of Spanish, or by acceptance of mediocre work due to inadequate knowledge and learning skills."

"We should upgrade the general education of island Salvationists?"

"Indeed. Augment their education generally and you will best equip them for Christian leadership."

It may well be that William Booth's unrealized dream of a University of Humanity may yet come true, in the paradise of the Atlantic—Puerto Rico, where, besides a general education, special attention could be given to the teaching of the humanities, plus attractive courses in Salvation Army history, music and other related subjects; and in Christian theology and Christianity in action. Salvationist youths who belong to the Corps Cadet program and Future Officers' Fellowship would attend day-time classes (some in a residential setting) and adults, evening classes plus seminars and symposiums. This would not prohibit non-Salvationist students from enrolling, but would emphasize quality education for the Salvationist.

Currently, under the direction of Brigadier and Mrs. Hazzard, the work includes 294 Senior Soldiers, 179 Junior Soldiers, 242 Home League members, 31 senior Local Officers, 25 youth Local Officers, 36 Future Officers' Fellowship members, 12 Nurses'

Fellowship members, 81 League of Mercy members, eight corps and other installations and one multi-welfare center.

The annual budget is met by mail appeals for camp and Christmas, unsolicited donations, *War Cry* selling, internal giving, the World Services Fund of the Eastern Territory, and the United Fund.

At present, programs are conducted in San Juan, La Perla, Rio Piedras, Loiza, Guayama, Ponce, Bayamon, Charlotte-Amalie, St. Thomas and St. Croix, with projected openings in several other cities and in the additional areas of day-care centers, senior citizen programs and rehabilitative work with prostitutes.

Puerto Rico has contributed twelve officers to Salvation Army ranks and there are many more young Salvationists who are contemplating officership.

REGIONAL HEADQUARTERS

This is in the process of being moved from the present cramped facilities, which will be used for a runaway program at Tetuan Street.[2] The regional staff is well-organized, hard-working, alert and eager; chief difficulties may well be inability on the part of some leaders to think and converse adequately in Spanish, and the financial burden of work that must be heavily subsidized.

SAN JUAN TEMPLE CORPS COMMUNITY CENTER

Lacking community-center recreational facilities, this is otherwise a lively operation with the usual complement of adult and children's activities, including women's Home League, Men's Club, youth activities, public meetings. A responsible group of Puerto Rican lay leaders take the ministry to the people, headed by Sergeant-Major Isaac Del Valle; Color Sergeant Angel Batista, who, though 81 years old, bears his tall self like a warrior in the front-line of battle; Jose de la Rosa, Recruitment Sergeant, whose workmates call him "preacher" and "Salvation Army." His daughter Iris recently was commissioned as an officer and he "is the happiest man in the world for this!" and Enrique Pagan, well-known as the Army collector in the San Juan area. He rejoices in collecting for "the Lord," and preaching, praying and handing out tracts along the way.

A leading member of the corps is Mrs. Hernan Fourquet who

assists with the Home League ministry in both this and the La Perla corps, directs the Girl Guard troop and is also part-time secretary of the Regional Commander.

Attracted by a street procession to the Caparra Temple corps was wide-eyed Eric Diaz, seven years old and captivated by the music and marching. Today, Eric, the first Junior Soldier to be enrolled in Puerto Rico (July, 1962), commands both San Juan Temple and La Perla corps.

SAN JUAN-LA PERLA CORPS COMMUNITY CENTER

The Salvation Army *War Cry* noted in 1968 that La Perla's poetic name "cannot hide the squalor and poverty of one of the oldest slums in the metropolitan area of San Juan."

Entrance and exit to La Perla are cut through the old city wall, and the sign warns: *NO VISITORS WELCOME.* This is not an understatement, though Salvationists, even strangers from the mainland, walk unhindered through the single street from which cement tributaries divide and re-divide like a human circulatory system. La Perla is always in motion. Even dogs, chickens and pigs ceaselessly dig.

"Ola! Ola!" come greetings as Diaz salutes a teenager, pats a naked baby, walks through an open door to greet a wrinkled old lady who needs spectacles (will the Lieutenant please see the man for her?) and a companion, middle-aged and retarded who gleefully displays a blond doll given her by The Army for Christmas. "Ola! Ola!" La Perla's swarthy leader (it does not have a mayor), Ramon Colon, sees the Lieutenant and, leaving friends, hurries over, greeting us, checking on forthcoming activities. A young builder ceases measuring wood siding for his reconstructed home as we approach. He shakes hands and says yes, his mother and family are all right. Yes, visit please.

"His older brother was murdered last week," Diaz says.

"You know them well?"

"The Joe Cuba family. I conducted his funeral."

"No other church connection?"

"They wanted somebody from the street."

I asked if there is police surveillance in La Perla.

"Ssssh," says Diaz. "Police come when called. Not one or

two—a dozen. Two dozen—with shotguns. The people aren't always happy about that."

We climb cement steps built for Paul Bunyan. Up and up and up, past dozens upon dozens of small cement-block or decaying wood housings, some disreputable and barren, others scrubbed and bright with paint. These people may be very poor, some illiterate, but they do not cry alone.

Children greet Diaz, women sweeping steps and sidewalks call, "Ola!" A young couple (the husband very thin and pale) thank him for the refrigerator and want to show him how it works.

Up. . . up. . . up. . .

At the Joe Cuba home an open door lets in ocean breezes that ruffle ceiling-to-floor, green-and-white drapes which soften the room. It is lined with folding chairs and backed by an alcove containing a battered refrigerator and a small table. On the white-clothed table are two tall glass-encased votives, a variety of icons and two photos of the dead man. Behind the table, from the ceiling hang about a dozen gold-embossed satin funeral streamers, assurances of neighbors' sympathy and reminiscent of county fair ribbons.

Diaz greets the mother and sister in Spanish. A wife and several children are also bereft. No, the son had no criminal record. There'd been an unplanned encounter regarding political views. A mainland musical recording was played. . . disagreement. . . a shot. . . explosive and tragic. Now, the streamers. Diaz preaches of Christian courage and fortitude, of marching on, supported by God's love. He prays. Both women smile softly, close their eyes. The mother holds her hands toward him in affectionate response.

The location of the Army's ministry in La Perla is clear. In the little Ejercito de Salvacion building, tucked among the people, offering recreational, educational and social welfare activities and services, yes; but more often, love's pulpit is predictably in the street.

Leaving La Perla, we pass Vivian's home, immediately distinguishable by a red Salvation Army shield to the left of the door. Vivian has full-time employment in the Army's San Juan thrift store. She is a pretty woman in her mid-thirties, her face lightly traced by sorrow. Destitute and disillusioned after her husband left her with three children, telling her that he had another wife and children, she came to live with a man in La Perla, in her words "a loose life." In a short time, however, she says she met a Friend who never forsakes. "Then my life was changed." She gave her gentleman friend an ultimatum: marry her or leave. He left, and Vivian was without support, emotionally and physically distraught and responsible for her children.

"I was soon all right," Vivian nods calmly. "Jesus took care of me." She continues, "Then I asked what can I do to help other people now?" She became a lay-assistant in the La Perla corps Home League, Sunday school and League of Mercy.

As we leave La Perla, Eric says the community center has called. There is urgent need for a pair of men's pajamas. Will the Lieutenant hurry over? The Lieutenant hurries, and so does his visitor.

"You certainly found those pajamas quickly. Hope they're not your own."

He grins. They are.

Funded by United States federal money, the La Perla community center is clean, commodious and well-equipped. Many old men sit about during our visit, chatting and readying themselves for craft work and dominoes. In one section, crafts are displayed; in another, about 30 sleek typewriters sit ready for "frf" and "juj." Youth activities are in evidence. The upstairs will soon become a day-care center. But the community center is outside La Perla's walls.

CAPARRA TEMPLE CORPS COMMUNITY CENTER

Today, Caparra Temple corps in Rio Piedras is a thriving corps community center, with a particularly active youth work. Especially active is a group of 44 older teen-agers called Torchbearers, recruited and directed by 17-year-old Enrique Vega, who envisions an army of youths who will effect an important contribution to Puerto Rico through the four-fold aim of the group: education, service, recreation and worship.

In command of the work are Sergeant and Mrs. Enrique Vega, and the story of their attraction to The Army and that of several other leaders begins with a change in the lives of Victor Ortiz and his wife, Sara. They will tell you it is all God's leading, a miracle.

One Sunday morning in 1964, returning to San Juan from New

York City, Corps Secretary Julio Santiago of the San Juan Temple corps, conversed with the man who sat beside him, Victor Ortiz, who worked in New York City and whose wife and children were visiting his mother in Rio Piedras (in which Caparra Temple corps is located). Santiago told him about The Salvation Army, and learned that Ortiz is a Christian with some Bible college background. As they left the plane, Ortiz promised to bring his family to visit the meeting that night. He did just that, bringing with him not only his wife but also five children to San Juan Temple. Later, the couple became lay members and leaders, and as Auxiliary-Captains took command of the San Jose corps. They were later trained as officers, and began a ministry which has led many people to Christ and the ranks of The Army, including the present commanders of the Caparra Temple corps, and Sergeants Ruben and Josefina Rodriquez, who now command the Bayamon corps. Their dedication has also resulted in the opening of a new corps-community center in nearby Loiza. Of the experience Ortiz says:

"God knows what He is doing. Most of my life I have followed Him. Some years ago in New York, there was a touch with The Army—only a touch but it lingered. With a vocal chorus I went to sing at the great Centennial Temple (Salvation Army worship center in New York City). I liked the joyful spirit of Salvationists and thrilled to hear the band. When I returned home after many years, my own church was not active locally so I sought out this Army. What I found so dear I thought my friends would too. That is how I came to invite them."[3]

Auxiliary-Captain Vega, present corps commander at Caparra Temple, had been invited by Ortiz to give a Bible message at the corps in 1970. He and his family became interested. A successful printer by trade, he'd worked on the mainland for 22 years and now was coming home, unsettled, but holding to the Scriptural promise that God would direct him. "I wanted to do something for God," reported Vega. "Now I want to march through the door that He opens."

The Vegas were approached regarding corps leadership by Major Leidy, then Regional Commander. Though trained only a month with the Ortizes before taking command in January, 1974, they have built a dynamic corps.

LOIZA CORPS COMMUNITY CENTER

For some time before January of 1974, Lieutenant and Mrs. Ortiz had conducted two outposts in Loiza, a rapidly expanding community about 25 miles from Rio Piedras and largely settled by low-income families whose sense of pride prods them toward self-help. At present, the Commonwealth provides modest parcels of land to citizens, on which cement blocks (provided by government funds) may be used to build little homes, often single-room dwellings, to be enlarged when funds and time permit. These are sturdy houses, usually brightly decorated and picturesquely landscaped by nature. Dogs, pigs, chickens and occasionally a horse are animate punctuations.

In January 1974, Loiza was dedicated as a corps though there was then no building to house the scores of adults and children who attended services and activities—no equipment, no flags, no drums, no uniforms—except those of the undauntable Victor Ortiz and his wife Sara.

"Sometimes I do not even wear the tunic (uniform jacket)," explained Ortiz, grinning. "You see, there we have no sidewalks and pavements, no playgrounds. I am in the street. And when I meet boys who wish to play ball off comes the tunic. . . . "

Corps activities are conducted in two dwellings, using carports as meeting-places, with the overflow spreading into street and other homes. There are two Sunday schools, two Sunday meetings, two Home Leagues, two Torchbearer brigades, two Sunbeam brigades and many more loosely structured activities.

The Loiza story is fascinating. About seven years ago a teenager, Carmen Pimentel, one of the first converts at the Caparra Temple corps (serving three years as corps assistant, then managing the Army thrift store), had for a customer a young high school electronics teacher. There was an immediate but respectful shock of interest in both. *"What is this, my Lord?"* prayed Carmen. *"I like this young man very much and I have never met him before. Oh please direct me. I must be very careful."*

Luis Davila asked whether it might be possible to have companionship. "May I date you?"

So.

"If you want to date me you'll have to attend my church," said

Carmen. Now he would see what kind of girl she was.

"Which one is that?"

"The Salvation Army."

Luis looked inquisitive. This lovely girl in an army?

"Very well."

He enjoyed himself at Caparra Temple. He also enjoyed himself in companionship with Carmen Pimentel and soon asked her to marry him.

"Oh. But if you want me to marry you, you'll have to become a member of my church."

Which he did. For some time Mr. and Mrs. Luis Davila were active in Caparra Temple Corps—Luis now taught a Bible class. But both felt the need to do something for God in their neighborhood, Mediania Alta.

Carmen and Luis approached Lieutenant Ortiz, then corps commander. Would it be all right to start a Sunday school in their home? They could use the carport. Soon, 30 to 40 children met weekly to pray and learn Bible stories taught by Luis.

"I remember," Ortiz recounted, "that during the summer of 1970 we chose 17 children from Loiza to attend summer camp at Aibonito. This, together with Mrs. Davila's interest, gave us our first Loiza Sunday schoolers. She herself taught for six months until responsibilities for her babies caused her to curtail her activities. Then, Arlene Valez took over. Arlene later got married and the Davilas went forward, inviting people in, going out and visiting their neighbors, using their home for a base of operations."

Many mothers became interested through their children. Was there some service they could have a part in? How could they help? Yolanda Pizarro started a Home League, visiting the neighborhood with Sara Ortiz. Next came Sunbeams. Something special going on at Caparra Temple? "Luis, we've got to take our people in. Ask the Lieutenant." Luis used his car. Ortiz used the station-wagon Loiza rolled to involvement.

Four years before, Carmen Davila had said to a friend of husband Luis, who was helping construct their cement-block home, "Here, take this paper and invite your wife to come to our Home League, will you?"

"Yes," said Pizarro. "I will. She will like to come here."

107 . . .

That was a significant piece of paper, for it interested Yolanda Pizarro, an engaging, buxom woman who now is lay leader at the other section of Loiza corps.

"I am happy in The Salvation Army," states Yolanda Pizarro. "I like all of it. I like the activities helping others. And I like the preacher." Her smile is infectious.

"How does it differ from that of others you've heard?"

"Oh, it is deep from the heart. Our Lieutenant means what he says. On Sunday he preaches. On Monday he is with the people."

The Pizarros had not long before returned to Puerto Rico from the mainland, where they'd lived for some years, so their six daughters might have a "more peaceful, moral and religious life and a better education" than New York's inner city provided. Four of their daughters have become cadets at the School for Officers' Training.

Yolanda became a Home League enthusiast and also began to attend Sunday services at Caparra Temple. The Lieutenant would bring a station-wagon for us on Sunday, but soon we wanted to go to The Army more than once a week, and the Lieutenant couldn't make more than one trip. It's quite a distance. So we asked if Ivett (one of the daughters) could start Sunday school in our carport. Then we could get to meeting more than once a week."

Recently, another daughter, Yolanda, saw a group of Sunbeams and said, "Lieutenant, can I do the same for Loiza? Can I begin Sunbeams?"

The necessary permission was given and 22 little girls attended the first Sunbeam meeting. Yolanda also took responsibility for the Torchbearer group of 15 members.

"An impressive story," we observed to Mrs. Pizarro. "Now you can help others."

"We do. This Christmas in Loiza we helped give. Christmas is how I met The Salvation Army."

"Oh?"

"Yes. On the mainland times were often bad. Christmas was bad. One Christmas we had actually nothing. My husband was out of work. No food, and a relative said to me, "Why not go to The Salvation Army? I hear they help anybody." I did not like going to ask for help but we were hungry. I didn't know about The Salvation Army and Jesus Christ. I just knew we were hungry. I went and I asked and they gave us food. Now I can be The Salvation Army to somebody else."

This is the beginning of the story of Loiza.

HOPE HOUSE MULTIPLEX WELFARE CENTER

Major Tobias Martinez, observing a need in old San Juan, instituted a hotel for transient men, partly in response to the need voiced by her honor, Mayoress Dona Felisa; and partly as a response to requests by local government officers. The charge was 25 cents per night, or four dollars per week for better accommodations, at 353 Calle Tetuan, later changed to 258 Calle Luna. The chief difficulty was that although some men and boys needed only a night's lodging, most needed care for much longer periods. Many were destitute, ill, in need of counsel and job assistance. They were unproductive and often unprotected in society, including runaways and ex-servicemen from the mainland, hippies, "cop-outs," probationers and parolees, alcoholics and addicts. Some needed long-term care; many, job opportunities and training. None of these services could be offered at the first Hope House.

Also, in 1963, when Major and Mrs. Churchill succeeded Martinez to the command of Puerto Rico, Churchill was quick to perceive two things: the need for better financing and a more effective program for needy men which would include a way to collect and distribute the public's material contributions, particularly clothing. Often, calls came from mainlanders now living on the island who knew of the Army's rehabilitative work of combining cast-off materials with cast-off men to help effect the reclamation of both. Would The Army pick up a bed, clothing, furniture, dishes? Churchill began to collect clothing in his car, pile it in a room until a need arose. Some things were immediately distributed to La Perla at the request of Captain Roberto Pagan, then commanding officer at San Juan Temple corps.

When Academia William Booth in Rio Piedras was judged an impracticable venture, part of the facility was retained for the Caparra Temple corps-community center, and part, in 1970, became the Hope House multiplex welfare unit. Each facet of the work outgrew its space, and in May of 1974 the work was relocated at Calle

Comercio 18, Ponce. Directing the welfare activities is energetic, amiable Captain Cesar Ferri with Mrs. Ferri, who also serves as Regional Guard and Sunbeam director. Captain Ferri is assisted by Franklin Machado and Bruce Fowler who is responsible for the center's corrections work. This was begun by Ramon Vasquez, the young man with the flute who in pioneer days attended one of Captain Gilberta Hess's meetings. Well qualified educationally, Fowler combines a preaching, counseling, family visitation and Bible study ministry in his contacts with inmates, actively engaged in work in the following correctional institutions:

>Princessa
>Mayaguez
>Ponce
>Guauate
>Punta Lima
>Guayama
>Oso Blanco

Included currently in the Hope House family are men of many kinds from many places—the ill-adjusted, middle-aged, the chronic alcoholic, parolees and probationers, a hippie who painted the center's fence a startling kaleidoscope of color, a disturbed Viet Nam veteran who can't face his family on the mainland—all in need of help.

Soon, visitors are aware of another person, not yet introduced. The men make referrals. Mothers wait. A phone rings incessantly. "See Elsa. Elsa will be with you in a moment. Elsa, phone!" Waiting your turn you see a curly dark head, and in front of the woman named Elsa, a Bible. A young man being interviewed has his back to you. He rises and you feel his gratitude. Elsa's duties combine intake and counseling for the men's social service work with family welfare casework, including the children and their families of the runaway program.

There is a pioneer feeling about the multiplex welfare center—eagerness, energy, faith. "It is like this," an employee said. "God wants mighty things to happen to His children. If Jesus is God, then He is timeless. Jesus is yesterday, today, forever. What happened by

Puerto Rican Cadets Welcomed by Comrades

SAN JUAN, P.R.—The four cadets of the Blood and Fire Session at the Puerto Rico extension of the Eastern Territory's School for Officers' Training were welcomed back by an enthusiastic crowd at the Temple Corps here recently.

The cadets and their training officer, Lieutenant Fidel Gonzalez, had attended orientation and welcome meetings in New York City. Mrs. Major Ralph Leidy, Regional Youth Secretary, presented them to the Regional Commander, Brigadier Lawrence Pickering.

The cadets gave a timbrel salute and gave their testimonies during a period of witness. Birgadier Pickering gave a charge to the new cadets.

Miguel Suarez, who attended the National Seminar of Evangelism for Soldiers this summer at Glen Eyrie, Colo., gave a report on the program there. Mrs. Major Leidy enrolled three new members of the Future Officers' Fellowship. Major Leidy, Regional Secretary, led a call to service, during which several persons committed themselves for officership in the future. The cadets attended their first officers' councils that afternoon.

Residence for the cadets this year will be on the third floor of the regional headquarters in Old San Juan. Mrs. Alvarez, mother of one of the cadets, from Montevideo, Uruguay, is serving as housemother.

The WAR CRY for November 13, 1971

Puerto Rico Corps Reports Full Hall, 21 Seekers

PONCE, P.R.—Just a year ago the Eastern Territory used some of its Self-Denial money to build a new 150-seat chapel for the Ponce Corps. Recently Captain Roberto Pagan, Commanding Officer, wrote a report of Candidates' Sunday meetings to Major Ralph Leidy, Regional Commander, stating that the hall was full of people and that 21 persons, mostly teenagers, had come forward at the close of the holiness meeting.

Young Marcus Hammalaunen, bandmaster, pianist and organist, gave the morning message. At night Corps Cadet Benson Laporte gave his first message. The teenagers led the way in commitment, both to future officership and to local evangelistic teams.

Captain Pagan summed up his reaction to the Sunday meetings in these words: "And the day ended in a spiritual evening that left us saying 'good-night' without wanting to leave the church, the house of God our Lord, but feeling inside our hearts, also the house of God, the fire of His holy touch and leaving inside our minds the pictures of this unforgettable day with the Lord."

The WAR CRY for April 22, 1972

Him and in Him can happen today—in us, by us."

Miracles in the multiplex center for the homeless and the hurt? That's what The Army is counting on.

PONCE CORPS COMMUNITY CENTER

Before leaving the command of Ponce in 1972, Captain and Mrs. Roberto Pagan built the multi-purpose corps community center Captain Shaffstall had envisioned. This is the first complex of Salvation Army buildings to be erected on the island and may serve as a pattern for other facilities. Succeeding the Pagans were Carlos and Emma Allemand, third-generation Salvationists trained in the Army's International School for Officers' Training in London. They brought many skills to the command, and were assisted in a quite remarkable youth program by a local Salvationist with an unusual story, university-taught Hernan Fourquet, Jr., known by close associates and hundreds of children and youths as "Junior." Besides directing the daily youth program, Junior was a lay leader in the Ponce corps. Why did such a man choose this work over a more scholarly profession?

Preceding his service for The Army, Junior had been director of the anti-drug program for the municipality of Ponce with several institutions under his control.

"I saw the flag in the open-air meeting when first The Army came to Ponce," Junior said. "I wondered about it. A flag is somewhat unusual. Militant. I wondered but I did not follow. Nothing persuaded me at that time—except the needle."

Son of a prosperous corporation manager in Ponce, Fourquet enjoyed advantages of home and education that many Puerto Ricans have not had. An accident to arm and leg when a teenager dropped him from star billing as an athlete to gross self-pity and failure. Gradually his grades went down, appreciation and acceptance of his family was dissolved and he "copped out." Other unfortunate incidents occurred, and by the time he had finished school and married, he felt revulsion for life. In an attempt to escape he flew to the mainland where he deposited himself and his agonizing drug habit in the vacuum of nonentity.

"Nothing, of course, was resolved." Fourquet's condition worsened. "Eventually I came back to find that The Salvation Army, through Captain Pagan, had been helping my wife and had become very important to her. I began to attend also."

Directed now by Sergeant and Mrs. Juan Jose Basualdo, who as lay leaders assisted Mr. and Mrs. Carlos Allemand, the Ponce corps now often knows "standing room only." It has a thriving youth corps, a brass band and is the home of Corps Cadet Marta Jusino, chosen in 1975 as territorial Corps Cadet of the year.

Ponce has many dedicated exemplary soldiers, and such a one is Angela.[4] Now a teacher, Angela and her daughter recently finished both high school and university together. Angela was a Christian, eager to participate in an active living experience of Christ but had stayed in seclusion due to the command of her husband. One day in June of 1973, she read a mimeographed invitation to help with the Ponce daily vacation Bible school. Volunteering, she taught children how to make crepe paper flowers. The children were excited and so was Angela. She liked this Army of peace. She attended a worship service. No doleful expression. No fear. No terrifying admonitions. "Jesus loves me this I know, for the Bible tells me so," the children sang. Soon, Angela was singing with them—regularly.

"Her husband advised her not to come," Carlos Allemand recalled, "but she intended not to lose what she had found. He beat her so badly, all down one side, damaging her ribs, that in desperation she left him to live in a nearby town. He visited me, saying he was sorry and wanted her back and would I help. I delivered the message, but Angela said she would not come back unless he allowed her to attend The Army. He agreed that she could come on Saturdays and Sundays—no more. She obeyed and all went well until not long ago when Angela became officially enrolled as a member of The Salvation Army. Delighted, she took home her Articles of War (statement of life commitment to Jesus Christ in the ranks of The Salvation Army), which concludes with the signer's promise to:

". . . spend all the time, strength, money and influence I can in supporting and carrying on the salvation war and that I will endeavor to lead my family, friends and neighbors and all others whom I can influence to do the same, believing that the sure and only way to remedy all the evils in the world is by bringing men to submit themselves to the government of the Lord Jesus Christ. . . "

Angela showed the document to her husband, who grabbed

and tore it, jeering, "You can't do this! You're no soldier!"

Angela became violently ill and was taken to the hospital, suffering a severe heart attack.

"Now she is being moved out of intensive care." The Salvationist smiled. "When we went to visit her last she said, 'Captain, I want you to visit across the hall. There is a woman who does not know Jesus. This is her name. . . .' "

In this manner grow the ranks of Christ's freedom fighters in Ponce.

SAN JOSE CORPS COMMUNITY CENTER

This little corps was started by a woman soldier of the San Juan Temple corps. She started taking neighborhood children to Sunday school with her own. The ministry grew so that she had to hire four taxis to transport her charges.

"This is ridiculous!" said Dona Petra. "Let's have Sunday school in my house." So she did. As soon as possible, Major Churchill, the Regional Commander, bought a little house in the neighborhood and appointed Captain Gilberta Hess as commanding officer. The meeting-hall-living-quarters arrangement is not uncommon in Puerto Rico, with patios and carports employed for congregations.

"Here, I lived with the people," notes Gilberta Hess Valentin. "And I think that's the secret of accomplishment for the Lord."

Arriving in San Juan from Ponce, Captain Hess was met by the Churchills.

"We've prepared the way for you. You'll see!" said Mrs. Churchill. "Gilberta, there's a young man of the area who's most interested in meeting the new captain. We've told him how lovely you are."

"The Lord had planned it all," remembers Gilberta. "Before the evening meeting, Carlos Valentin was the first person I saw. Later, I enrolled him as a soldier. And yes, I married him."

However, the brightness of the days to come was not apparent the first night. It was a most distressed area of the city, among project buildings, and Gilberta had been told how dissolute it was.

"Sin really abounded in San Jose and was everywhere evident. Drug use was common, and the buying and selling of it. Children not only had filthy bodies but also used indescribable language. Other conditions were shocking. For example, I remember a woman later to become a respectable Home League member who used to put out a blanket in front of her home and entertain her men friends there. That first night I thought, 'Here I am all by myself. No assistant. Not even my dog.' "

She locked her door and went to bed. About three o'clock a.m. there was a pounding on the door and a woman's voice crying, "American! American! Please come and help me!"

Gilberta leaped up, pulled on her uniform and rushed to the door. There stood a distraught woman.

"My daughter! My daughter she has set herself on fire!"

They ran to the home, where the 21-year-old daughter was in a terrifying condition. She'd gotten upset, poured gasoline on herself and lit a match. Gilberta drove her to the hospital and stayed with the family through the night.

"We watched through the night, seeing her skin coming off in black sheets. All I could do was stay, praying with the family for courage, until she died about five hours later. I'll never forget her screams."

Gilberta's concern, however, opened wide a door to the heart of San Jose, for the people knew now there was a door to knock on when they were in need.

Experiences often included encounters with grief and pain, but few compared with the horror Gilberta felt when one day a favorite friend was stricken. She'd noticed the little boy from her first Sunday school meeting. Always he would sit at her feet and listen but seldom participated. "He seemed so special," remembers Gilberta. "One day in the project where he lived, other children put him in a garbage can among many others and set him afire." It was a long time before another child could rescue him. He lingered between life and death for weeks, but through the aid of The Army and Gilberta's parents, Brigadier and Mrs. Gilbert Hess, who served on the mainland, the little boy was taken to Boston, where he underwent 10 operations and eventually recovered.

The people of San Jose opened their hearts, and they came to Army meetings which were held in the quarters' carport. In this busy street community pandemonium was the usual substitute for a quiet worship hour, yet, relates the former corps officer, "Holiness meetings were such blessed times. Even though jets interrupted the sermons, a crowing rooster regularly practiced his art during meeting, the man next door hammered away on reconstruction and passing cars screeched by, it was great! God was there and God's creatures were there and the noise of the world didn't disturb us because He was speaking."

Soon, 75-100 San Josians gathered to share praise to God in the carport, and besides being a place of worship, the San Jose quarters became an after-school haven for children, for women of the Home League and for the brokenhearted.

Due to lack of leadership, the San Jose corps was closed, an action regretted by many.

GUAYAMA CORPS COMMUNITY CENTER

In this nature-festooned city of 40,000 persons, Lieutenant and Mrs. Felipe (Daisy) Machado, first officers to be commissioned in Puerto Rico, conduct a singular ministry among central community residents and those of Grandstand, an outlying area of shacks which house about 50 families—300 persons. Compared to that, many believe La Perla is a country-club community. Here, visitors don't seek a welcome, not even the mailman. Mail is left outside the community at a nearby tavern. Because the trails have no names, the people have no addresses.

Lieutenant Machado commented, as we arrived, "When we first started Sunday school here, the children knew only their given names. So, in order to visit their homes Daisy and I walked through the village, knocking on doors and asking, 'Is there a little boy so high named Jorge here? A little girl named Rosa?' Last summer at daily vacation Bible school we gave prizes for coming clean."

Here come the cast-offs, the derelicts, the shunned, the old and others who are altogether bereft of hope. Here has sprung up a strange community. It is an easily infested area. In the stream at their back door Grandstanders throw refuse, bathe, swim, fish and wash clothes, and their animals lounge. Their shack squares are fenced and topped with barbed wire; and beside the doors of most are religious symbols—crosses, hex signs, peace symbols, weed and grain decorations "to keep the evil spirits away." If the rain is not heavy, mud paths are negotiable.

"Will we be intruding?"

"Oh no," said Daisy, nodding. "This is our appointment. Come see our building."

Made available to The Army by the city of Guayama without cost are two single-room, cement-block structures, one of which the people will not enter because it had been the home of lepers, and later, tuberculosis patients. When patients were judged incurable or dying, and the nearby municipal hospital was overcrowded, they were put in such buildings, which have no doors or windows—just openings—and a local woman was paid to feed and minimally tend them. At one time withdrawn, food was again distributed at the plea of the Machados.

We walked on, carefully picking our way between rocks, refuse and dung. Felipe and Daisy greeted everyone. How is the new baby? Is the husband up and about? The burned hand? Watch the dog! Be careful. Don't slip on the dung. Bony little dogs everywhere and children... very friendly children. A man reels by, respectfully nodding. The Machados greet him and stop the children who follow him, heckling.

"Is there electricity?"

"Very few have it," Machado says, "nor water, which is piped to the edge of the community and there is a faucet by the roadside. Most of the clothes washing and bathing is done in the creek though. Hello! How are you?" They greeted an elderly man wearing clean clothes and very large dark glasses. The greeting was cordial except for a certain reserve. Turning toward the corps building, we realized he was still watching.

"He is a spiritist," explained Daisy. "When we first came he was very interested and asked us for a New Testament but he has been removed lately."

We asked about spiritism. There is great dependence on the spirit world, inhabited both by evil and good... there are incantations... magic potions... a variety of denunciations... anathema. We walked on. Nearing the Army building, we met Rosa, visited in the cubicle she calls home. Old and ailing but spicy—Rosa. "Down!" She glared at two small dogs. "Down!" So happy for visitors. Daisy chatted with her as a Home League member. She can't go outside

117 . . .

because her legs are too unsteady for the rough paths. No, no family near... a son went to the mainland years ago... she wishes she could find him... she wishes she could go live in some nice place for old people... sometimes it's frightening here... at Christmastime vacationing boys from the reformatory robbed people and burned trees near Grandstand.

There are many pictures of Jesus on her walls.

In the open door next to Rosa sat a staring woman, her right arm extended upward. "She doesn't move for long times. I think she is sick."

Then to the Army building. Two identical structures. The children congregate. "Ola! Ola!" Inside one of the cement cubes is a miniature Salvation Army hall—painted, clean, a pulpit and folding chairs. There are a few programs from last Sunday, announcements of coming events on the bulletin board.

"Difficult to work here right now," Machado said. "Drug addicts who used next door as a shooting gallery cut the wires. We wish there were a bigger building."

"And, oh there is so much need," says Daisy. "How they need the Master who would change them so well. And they would change their surroundings. But they do not seem to understand. They do not listen long, and they do not seem to remember. If only there were some other ways besides the preaching to tell the message."

"Perhaps," said a visitor, "the pulpit is not the beginning. Maybe God has another, better way. Who knows? And it is good to remember that above all else, *you* are His message to them."

How do such ministries begin? In 1971 a letter went from a woman in Guayama to headquarters, asking The Salvation Army to come to her city and begin work. The invitation proved not to be acceptable; nevertheless, in the summer of 1972, when a group of young Salvationists from the Eastern Territory spent the summer in Puerto Rico, 10 days were spent in Guayama for plaza open-air meetings, planned when Major Leidy and Captain Pagan visited Guayama's mayor, Sr. Victor Borrero, who seemed exceedingly grateful for the interest. He had, he said, known about The Army on the mainland.

"I want to meet your group," he said. "I'll take the whole bunch to lunch tomorrow." At lunch, the Army's initial work in

Puerto Rico was outlined, together with Leidy's hopes to establish work in towns such as Guayama and make the work self-supporting. How could The Army best serve Guayama?

"Look," the mayor said, "I want to show you an area in which I'm much interested and where I think The Army can work best."

The area was Grandstand.

Needs in Grandstand are ongoing, but results are spectacular. To date, Sunday school, Home League, League of Mercy, camp and welfare work have been effected, with emphasis on prayerful home visitation. And baseball. Do not forget baseball. During the summer flood of 1973, Machado and his father carried the people out to a schoolhouse, many of them stubbornly resistant. Children have been taken to summer camp. Now Grandstanders stand up, smile when Felipe and Daisy Machado come neighboring.

Waiting for us as we turned to make a trailway exit were dogs and children. . . older teenagers staring from steps. . . the drunken citizen again. . . an impeccably groomed teenage girl who says her five-year-old daughter is "first to Sunday school and last to leave," the spiritism gentleman looking like a sentinel. . . and Luis.

Luis is 14, healthy and handsome, his head covered with a knitted cap because his haircut is too short, with an adventuresome look in his black eyes. The Machados conversed in Spanish with him. He grinned, shook hands. Luis always helps the Lieutenant I was told. Luis is a good student in the ninth grade, reading and reading. The Machados explained that the house across the way would be so much better for a hall, having several rooms. But when the owner was questioned he wanted $16,000. Luis lives in the house with his grandmother.

"She's not my grandmother!" said Luis in Yankee English. "I just live with her."

"Luis" we said. "You speak English!"

Merriment in his eyes. Big joke.

"You learned in school?"

"Yes."

"You like to learn? To read?"

"Yes."

"Sports?"

"I like baseball. I like also to fish."

"Would you like me to send you some books?"
Luis glowed. "Yes."
We shook hands, laughing, sharing what cannot be spoken.
Now the spiritism man stood beside his fence, his door wide open. There was a small clean table with scissors and combs and a mirror, and a multi-colored statue of an American Indian. A boy of about seven patted him and ran—his son.
"He is the barber," Machado said. "He says he had a very sad time until two years ago when he moved here. These have been the happiest years of his life."
"Ask him if he still has his Testament."
"He says he is very interested in God and Jesus, studies a lot. When he got his Testament he carried it in his shirt pocket. But when he went to the spiritism meeting he buttoned it inside his jacket so no one would know. As he stepped inside the door, the leader, a woman, began to jump and scream at him and the Testament burned him until he had to open his jacket and throw it out. Then the people threw him outside. Now he lets the meetings be held in his house so peace will prevail. But he is interested in God and Jesus."
"Ask him what he did before—his occupation."
"He says he was a baseball player, a professional."
So.
"Ask him what position he played."
The man made a throwing gesture and smiled.
"He was a pitcher."
"Good!"
Machado asked if he would help with a ball team if equipment were provided.
"Yes."
One last pause. Behind us little boys were wildly beating on cans in an abandoned block house, singing farewell. A startlingly familiar tune. "And when the battle's over, we shall wear a crown." Felipe and Daisy waved, repeating the words:
"With Jesus in the family, happy, happy home;
Happy, happy home;
With Jesus in the family, happy, happy home;
Happy, happy home."
Soon after, the city of Guayama made available to The Salva-

tion Army a large building near Grandstand, formerly the city jail. Welfare work could now be directed from it.

In November, 1975, we paid another visit to Guayama and were astounded to observe the successful embattlement of the corps. Only Divine guidance can account for the changes.

Certainly, the personal living conditions of Felipe and Daisy and their small children have not been much altered. They still hold all services next to the abandoned leper house. Their minute living quarters overflows with Salvation Army office and service paraphernalia, including a shield-stamped urn for emergency and disaster service which sits on top of Felipe's file cabinet, and Daisy's League of Mercy kits blocking the corridor from living to bedroom. The abandoned jail, unrenovated, accommodates the thriving welfare work but is stonily unappealing, though the Machados talk glowingly of the possibility of converting the entire structure one day into a center for worship, community services and counseling rooms.

In the long-empty courtroom with provocative art on clammy walls and the lathed ceiling revealing mostly Puerto Rican sky, they describe the meetings-to-be, and enthusiastically count invisible worshipers who can be squeezed in, hallelujahing "So beautiful!"

The Machados tell a strange story: The former baseball pitcher (the spiritist) kept his word, and so did young Luis, who publicized the baseball invitation. Felipe immediately approached the mayor who, with two other businessmen, personally contributed money for baseball uniforms, bats, balls, and a catcher's mask. The team was entered in the Guayama Little League (11-13 age group) and won its first game 16 to 4. Winners all the way.

When the Army's 1973 summer encampment was planned, the boys were invited to attend; however, some mothers were reluctant to let their children go with strangers. Personal visits were paid to the mothers by the Machados and the mothers were invited to attend the Home League. Luis' mother became the first Home League member and is now a soldier. When Guayama was allowed to take additional youngsters to camp, the Machados took along 40. The camp was especially fortunate in having two young sergeants, Mr. and Mrs. Ruben Rodriquez, assigned to counsel the children spiritually, and during the camp 34 of the 40 gave their hearts to Christ and upon return asked parental permission to attend The Salvation Army.

"We don't know about The Salvation Army. You cannot join."

Whereupon, the boys begged the Machados to visit their homes. More Papas and Mamas investigated the militants who do not use violence. And suddenly, the Machados tell you, "Our place was full! We could not find room and often hold our meetings now outside the hall."

This is part of the story. One-third.

Another centers in Guayama welfare work. As the spiritual ministry grew, Felipe realized he could not cope. "I found I had no time for the social work. I had to shepherd the people."

But again, in the course of everyday duty, the answer came. Through a Christian message given by Daisy in the local jail, a university-trained inmate was converted and began to witness to his cellmates. Because many of the men were not literate, he had a special ministry in letter writing for them. Later, he was paroled to The Army, with his salary paid by the city and made welfare worker in the old jail. Incredible? What's more, he often accompanies the Machados to jail meetings, giving invaluable witness and counsel.

Still there is more. The most important part. The Machados had come to Guayama from an appointment in the San Juan Temple corps where, just graduated from the School for Officers' Training, eager but inexperienced, they threw themselves into corps duties in a self-consuming manner which left little time for home life or personal spiritual growth. Felipe often left home early in the morning to be gone till midnight, and Daisy was left with her share of official duties and also the care of three babies.

"When we came to Guayama," explained Felipe, "we knew we had been responsible for too much. We were not well enough trained. We had forgotten our peace in God. We were so unhappy. And such need was everywhere."

"But here, in this beautiful city, we found calm in our quiet," continued Daisy. "At first, we thought to leave The Salvation Army. We thought maybe we couldn't work in it. Next, we thought maybe, as we prayed on, we could change The Salvation Army. And now, we know that God has charge of The Salvation Army—and of us. That is what the problem was all about. We were the ones who needed to change, to realize we could not effectively, happily, be in charge of ourselves or anyone else. Now, He has a dwelling-place inside us.

Now, we do not fret over how to get things done, how to get people to know our Lord. We just simply let Him lead."

Felipe smiled. "God does a very good job. He does it better than our best efforts." *That* is the Guayama story.

> *Blessed Saviour, now behold me*
> *Waiting at Thy bleeding feet;*
> *In Thy mercy breathe upon me,*
> *Make me for Thyself complete.*
>
> *Breathe upon me, even me,*
> *Make me what I ought to be;*
> *In Thy mercy breathe upon me,*
> *Make me for Thyself complete.*
> —WILLIAM BAUGH

Notes

1. "We would need to prove ourselves to the people with our work, before assurance could be forthcoming from her city government. If it proved that our work was being done for the people's good and to meet a need, there would be no question that our work would receive every consideration for financial support...." Excerpt from Martinez letter to Eastern Territorial Headquarters, USA, 1961.

2. Youth Home to alleviate the immediate problems of runaway youths during the runaway episode by providing them with shelter and food while a social worker has an opportunity to work on the possibility of either reuniting them with their families, if this is desirable, or to make other permanent arrangements for them. Previously, local runaway youths who came to the attention of the police had no place for temporary shelter until their problems could be resolved.

3. At the time this book is being written, Sara Elsie, daughter of Captain and Mrs. Ortiz, is a Cadet in the Eastern Territorial School for Officers' Training.

4. Fictitious name.

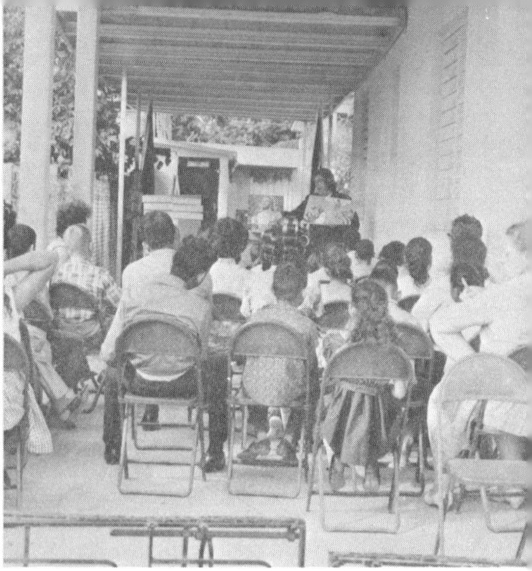

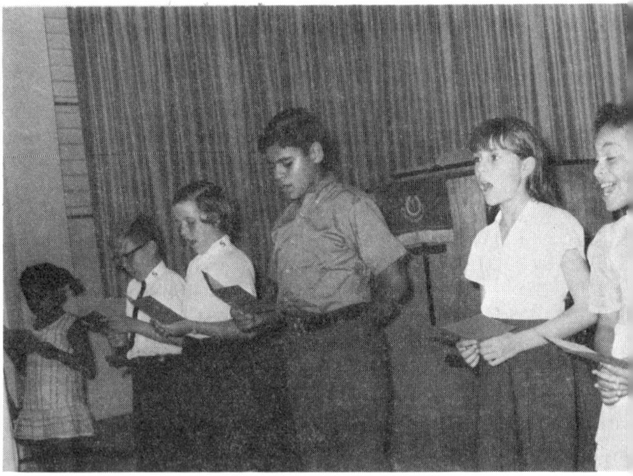

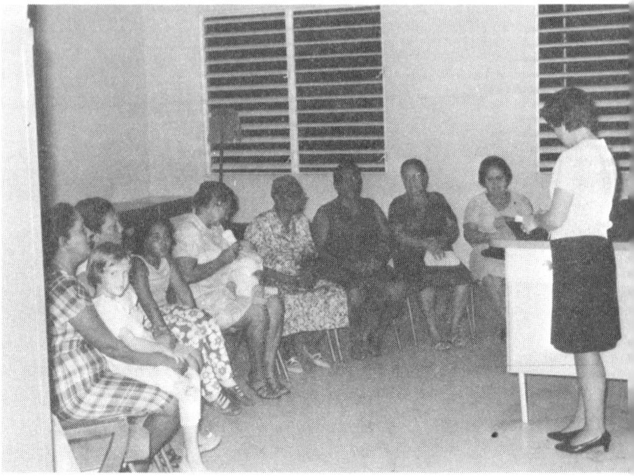

Puerto Rico

Puerto Rico

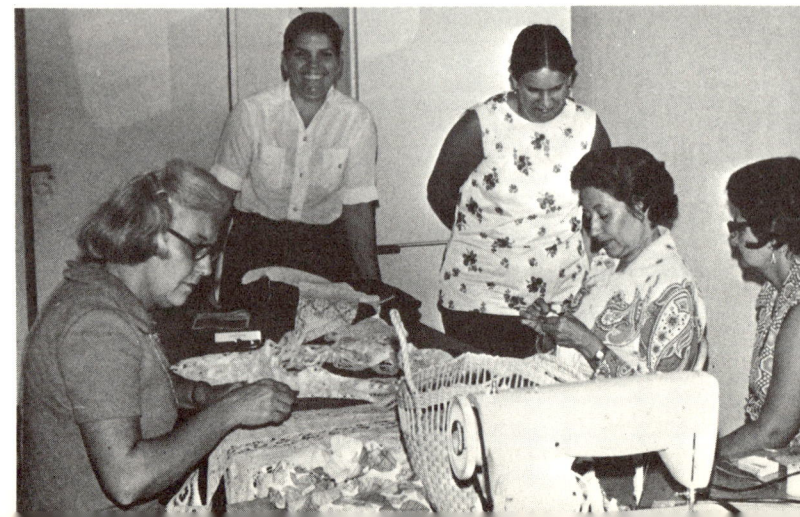

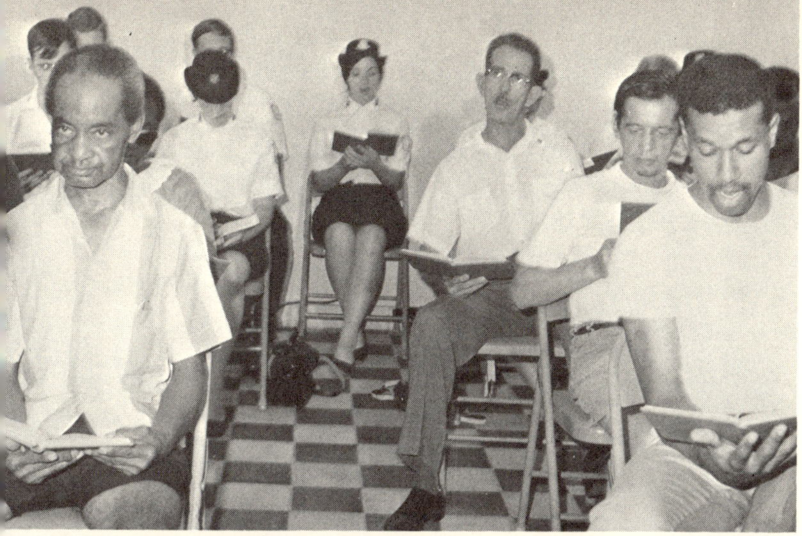

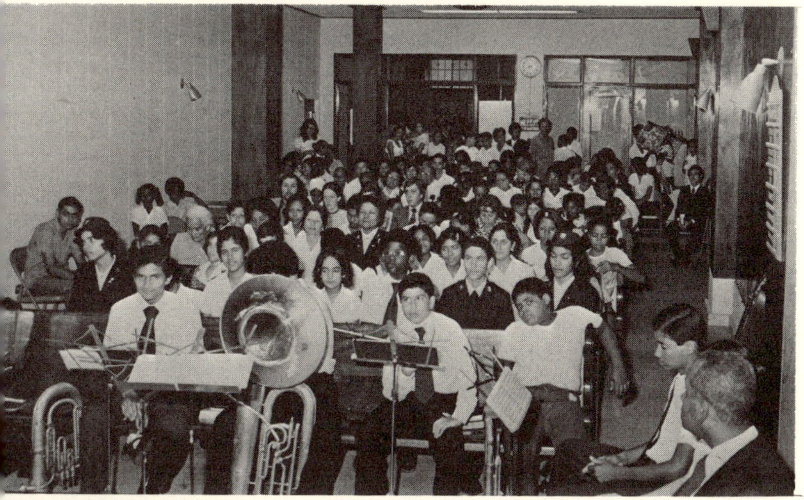

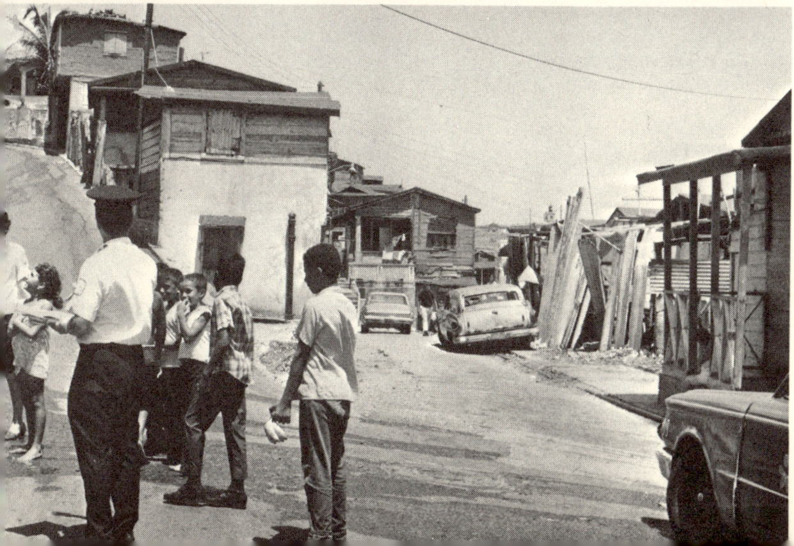

Puerto Rico

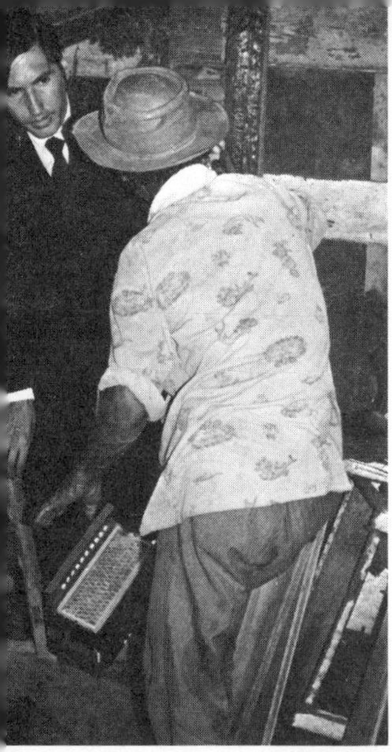

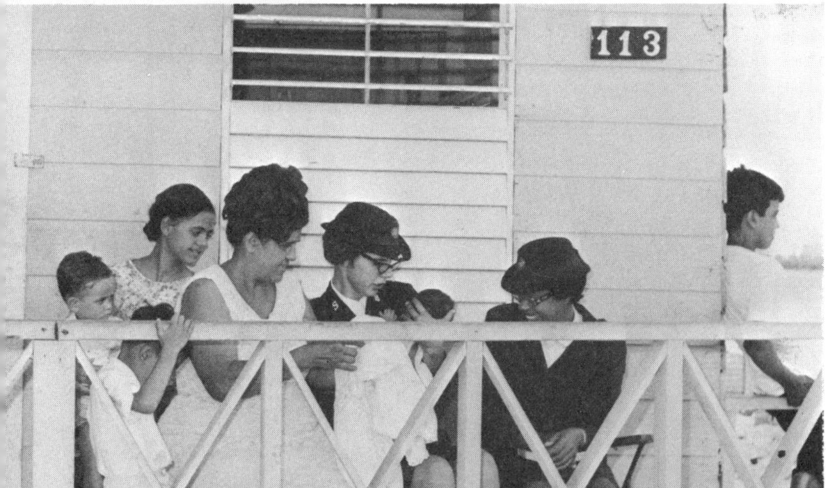
113

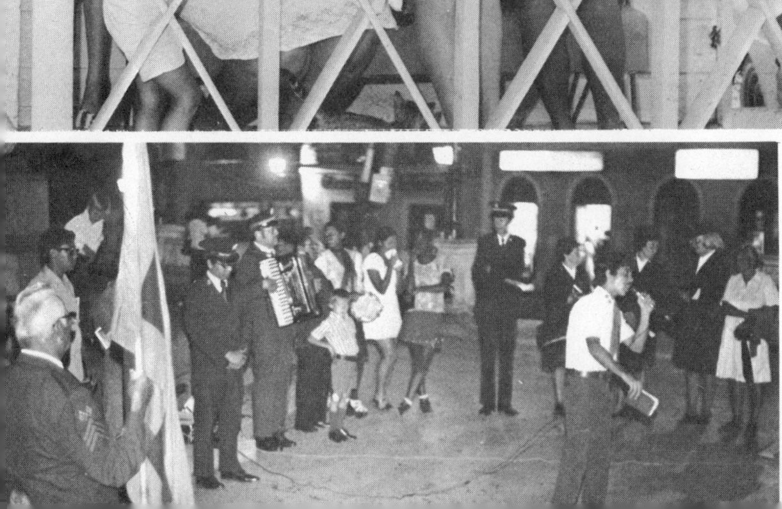

*I'll go in the strength of the Lord
In paths He has marked for my feet;
I'll follow the light of His Word,
Nor shrink from the dangers I meet;
His presence my steps shall attend,
His fulness my wants shall supply;
On Him, till my journey shall end,
My unwav'ring faith shall rely.*

*I'll go in the strength of the Lord
To work He appoints me to do;
In joy which His smile doth afford
My soul shall her vigor renew.
His wisdom shall guard me from harm,
His power my sufficiency prove;
I'll trust His omnipotent arm,
And prove His unchangeable love.*

—EDWARD TURNEY

CHAPTER IV

March On!

"QUE PASA? QUE PASA?"
 Always this is the question when The Salvation Army marches into town.
 In November, 1975, under the direction of the Regional Commander, Brigadier William Hazzard, with Mrs. Hazzard, the first Monday Evening at the Temple (San Juan) was conducted with a crowd from all island installations. So large was the congregation that it spread out the rear doors and across Tetuan Street.
 The jubilant occasion was preceded by an open-air service in which about 150 persons sang, testified, spoke from Scripture and prayed, the kind of street meeting the Salvation Army's founder, William Booth, would have exulted in. Captain Samuel Eliasen, Divisional Youth Secretary, and Mrs. Major Mario Jourdan, Regional Home League Secretary, translated, and the Captain led the service. Program items included: brass instrumental numbers by the Ponce band; vocal selections by the united chorus; testimonies by Captain Victor Ortiz and Corps Cadet Marta Jusino. The Corps Cadet had that day been featured in the San Juan paper for having

been chosen Corps Cadet of the Year. During the Eastern Territory's Heritage Horizons Congress in October, 1975, before 5,000 cheering Salvationists in the Felt Forum, General Clarence D. Wiseman had presented a scholarship to the Corps Cadet.

Enthusiastic guests from Territorial Headquarters for the occasion were Colonel Howard Chesham, Secretary for Business for the Eastern Territory, and Mrs. Chesham. The service was patterned after the renowned New York Friday Evening at the Temple. At the conclusion, the penitent-form was lined with penitents and seekers after a Spirit-filled life. Among the seekers was a young prostitute, garbed for the street. She knelt among uniformed young people and tearfully assented to the offer of the welfare director to find housing for her, away from the street.

Angeline Hernandez, secretary to Ray Owen, manager of radio station WAPA, will be glad, for The Salvation Army appears to be helping Puerto Rican pride increase as islanders turn to Christ. Happily, it has had a part in encouragement, assistance and celebration. Also, there is accumulative proof that the measure of free people, as Angie stated, is "one hand upon another."

From where comes the trust to accept this powerful, prodding intimacy? Ruben, Victor, Elsa, Ramon and Franklin, Rosa, Luis, Pedro, Enrique, Juanita, Angela, Mercedes, Yolanda, Carmen, Felix and Mildred, Vivian and Benjamin, Eric and Arcadia will tell you, "It is Christ who makes the person personal, loving and trustworthy. When He comes, the people understand. The people accept."

God's power to His people in Puerto Rico and the Virgin Islands! And to His people everywhere.

Thou shalt know Him when He comes;
Not by anything He wears;
Not by His crown,
Nor His gown;
But His coming known shall be
By His holy harmony
That His presence makes in thee.

—ANONYMOUS

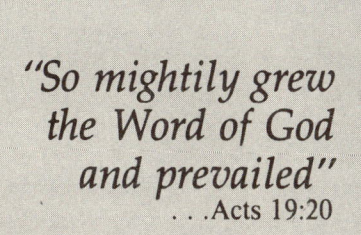

"So mightily grew
the Word of God
and prevailed"
. . .Acts 19:20

PUERTO RICO

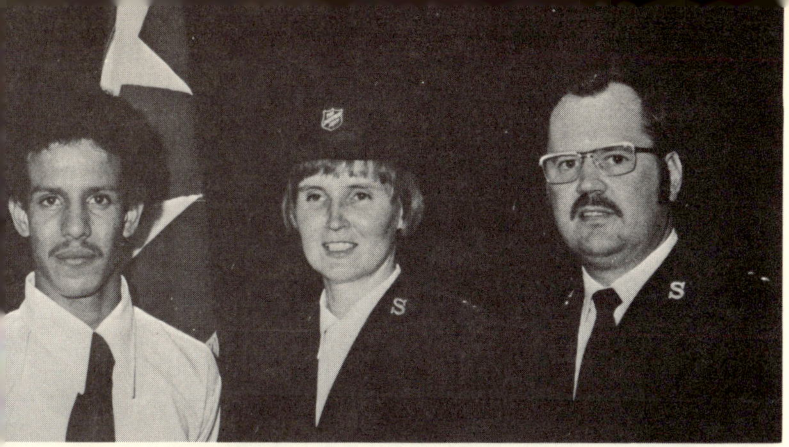

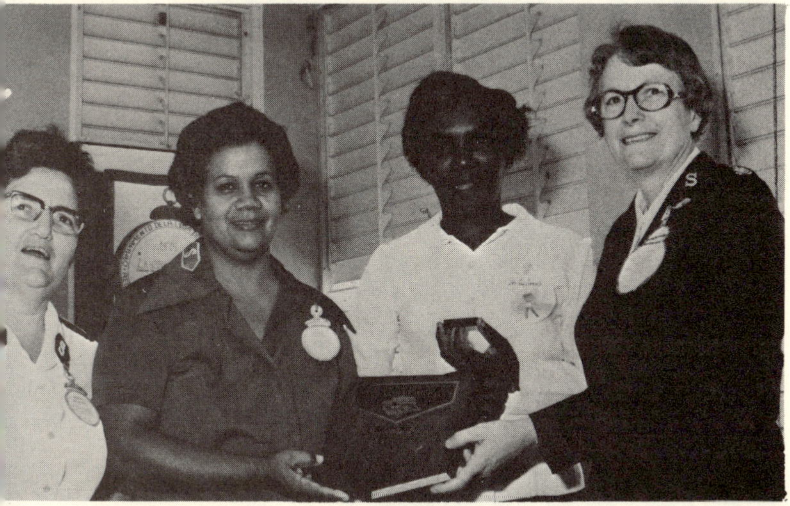

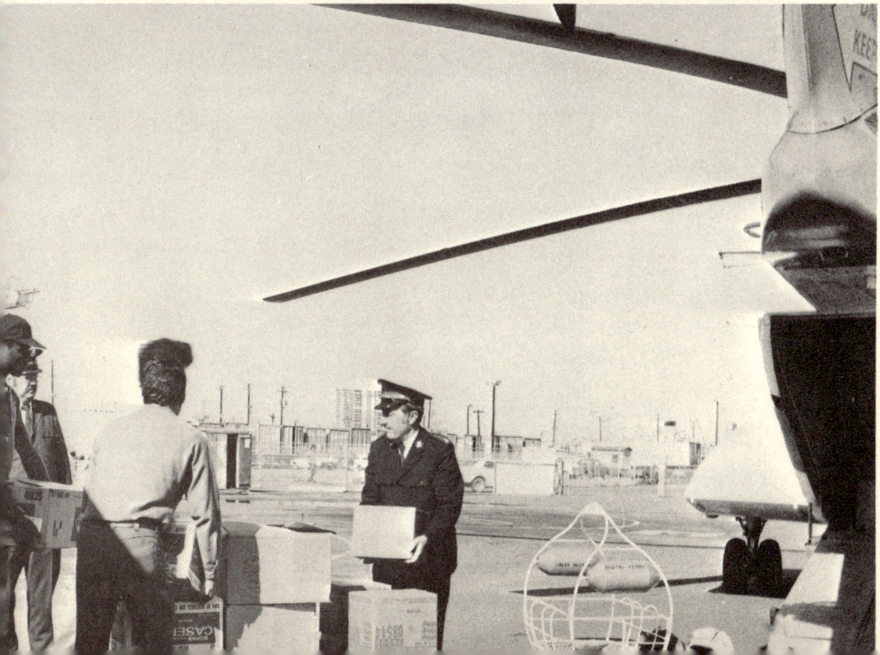

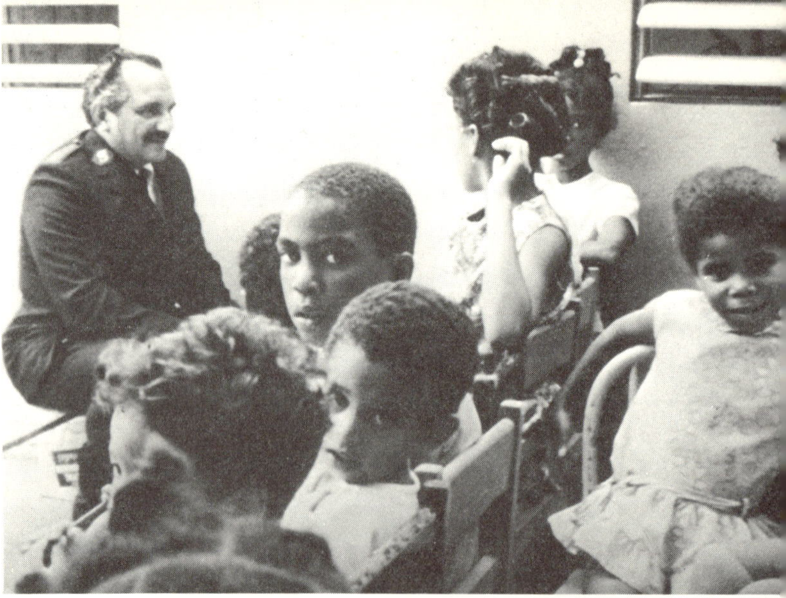

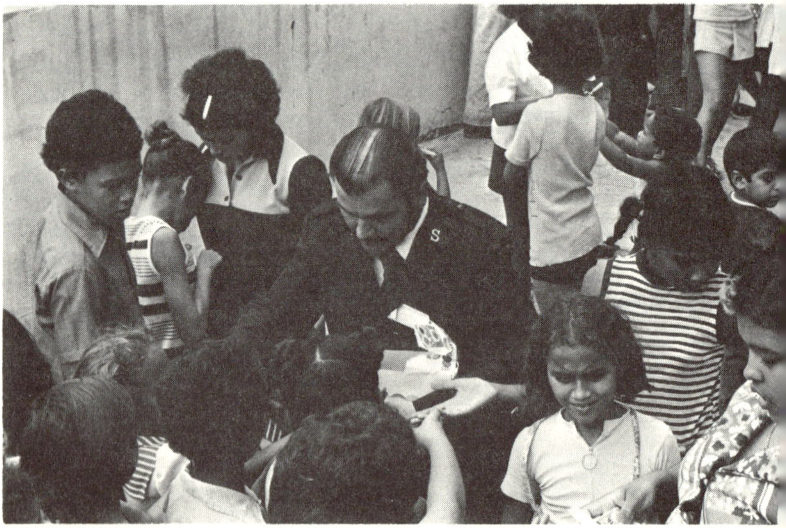

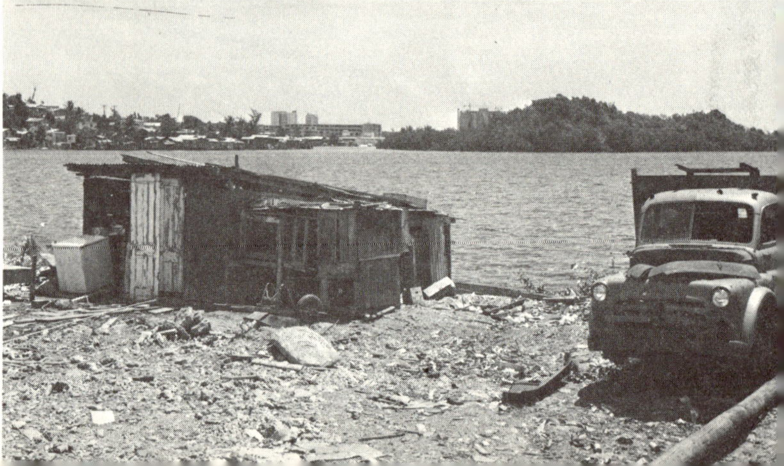

PUERTO RICO

DEFINITION OF SALVATION ARMY TERMS USED IN
ONE HAND UPON ANOTHER

ADHERENT: A person of good standing and character who considers The Salvation Army to be his place of worship by attendance and financial support.

BAND: A group of Salvationists who voluntarily serve together to further the purposes of The Salvation Army by means of instrumental music. Bands provide opportunity to render Christian service in many areas of Salvation Army activity. Instruction and assistance in the development of musical interest are services provided to members by band leaders. Bands are comprised of both adult and youth members.

CADET: A trainee for officership in a Salvation Army School for Officers' Training.

CANDIDATE: A person called of God who has offered himself for officership in The Salvation Army.

CASEWORK: Social casework is a method used by qualified social caseworkers in The Salvation Army to help individuals to find solutions to their problems of social adjustment which they cannot deal with by their own efforts. Casework is based on respect for human personality, belief in the individual, his uniqueness and his capacity to develop and adjust.

CHRISTMAS KETTLE: A receptacle with an identifying sign used during the Christmas season by The Salvation Army for the collection of funds for services to needy persons.

CORPS: The corps (in some communities referred to as a neighborhood center) is the basic unit of The Salvation Army. Under the direction of a commissioned officer who administers both religious and welfare activities, the corps is the center for a varied program which includes regular religious services, evangelistic campaigns, pastoral counseling, institutional and family visitation, character-building activities for youth, and such social welfare programs as are directed by the needs of the community in which the corps is located. The total corps program of religious and social welfare work implements the Army's purpose of preaching the Gospel and effecting the spiritual, moral and physical reclamation of persons coming under its influence.

CORPS CADET BRIGADE: An organized corps group activity for Salvation Army young people (7th grade students or over) through which is provided a six-year course of study including Bible, Salvation Army organization, doctrine and history designed to prepare young Salvationists for future leadership within the organization.

CORPS COUNCIL: A council established within the local corps of The Salvation Army to advise and assist the commanding officer on matters concerning the progress and well-being of the work under his command.

CORPS OFFICER: An officer in command of The Salvation Army local corps.

CORPS WELFARE SERVICES: The Salvation Army corps welfare program is designed to provide emergency help for distressed people, regardless of race or creed, whose need is brought to the Army's attention either by referral or direct contact. The scope of the service is determined by the needs of the community and available resources. In communities where there are no specialized institutional services or no central welfare department, the corps welfare program may be expanded to include family service, transient service, emergency shelters, missing persons service, and Christmas as well as other seasonal welfare activities.

CORRECTIONAL SERVICES: The Salvation Army as a voluntary agency works cooperatively with prison, probation and parole officials, and with judges in many courts—Federal, State and local—to augment, wherever possible, their efforts toward rehabilitation and crime prevention. Services to prisoners include Bible correspondence courses promoted by chaplains and other prison officials; employment opportunities in cooperation with parole personnel; spiritual and material aid to prisoners and their families. In addition, Salvationists regularly conduct services in jails and prisons and observe a nationwide Salvation Army Correctional Services Sunday on a yearly basis.

EDUCATION AND TRAINING OF OFFICER PERSONNEL: Four schools for Officers' Training are maintained by The Salvation Army in the United States to provide for the education and training of officer personnel. These schools are located at the four territorial centers as follows: Atlanta, Chicago, New York, San Francisco. The Salvation Army officer must be trained to assume his role in the community. The accelerated and intensive in-residence course of two years' basic training provided at the School for Officers' Training equips the officer to conduct the religious and welfare programs for which the Army is responsible. This period of training is preceded by high school and/or college, and also by preparatory studies for periods ranging from one to six years in the local corps. The curriculum at the training school covers Bible study, doctrine, Salvation Army and church history, leadership training, music, social studies and other related subjects. Graduation from the School for Officers' Training is followed by three to five years of directed study and supervised in-service training related to the specific work of the officer. The Army's system of education also provides opportunity for further training in such specialized fields as religious education, medicine, hospital administration, nursing, accounting and social work.

EMERGENCY DISASTER SERVICE: Through the Emergency Disaster Service, trained Salvationists and volunteer personnel provide food, housing, clothing, counseling and spiritual comfort to disaster victims to the extent that resources are available.

EMERGENCY LODGE: A home in which The Salvation Army provides food and lodging for women and children during a period of crisis. The most frequent users of Emergency Lodge services are persons in the following categories: families evicted from their homes, or dislodged because of fire or other disaster; families broken by desertion; newcomers stranded in a city. Individuals are received into the home through referral from various community social agencies, police, firemen, or by their own request. Length of stay is determined on an individual basis according to need.

EMERGENCY RELIEF: The assistance given in an emergency to an individual or family, including food, shelter, clothing and counseling.

GIRL GUARDS: A non-denominational organization established by The Salvation Army for girls from 10 through 18 years of age, who subscribe to a program which promotes good character and good citizenship; develops proficiency and skills in subjects related to care and development of the body, mind, soul; encourages service to others; and teaches and encourages Christian living.

HARVEST FESTIVAL: A commemoration in the autumn season during which Salvation Army soldiers and interested friends give a thank-offering, and appropriate services are planned.

HOME LEAGUE: An organization within a Salvation Army corps or institution for all women (16 years of age and over), the purpose of which is fourfold: to improve skill and develop mental culture (education); to learn to know more of God and His will (worship); to share in Christian comradeship (fellowship); to learn the joy of giving to others and serving their needs (service).

JUNIOR SOLDIER: A Salvation Army lay member between 7 and 14 years of age.

LEAGUE OF MERCY: A volunteer group of Salvationists and interested friends who regularly visit in hospitals, homes for the aged, prisons, children's homes, and mental institutions, cooperating with institutional authorities in providing spiritual and social therapy for the clients.

LOCAL OFFICER: A lay member of The Salvation Army who has been placed in a position of leadership in a local corps.

MEN'S FELLOWSHIP CLUB: An organization within The Salvation Army corps which provides a program for men, the purpose of which is to promote friendliness and good fellowship, to stimulate interest in community service and through various service projects for youth to contribute to the moral and spiritual welfare of boyhood.

MEN'S SOCIAL SERVICE CENTER: A Salvation Army center which is open to men with social, emotional, and spiritual needs who have lost the ability to cope with their problems and as a result have become economically unable to provide for themselves. The center provides adequate housing with work and group therapy in clean, wholesome surroundings. Physical and spiritual care prepare the beneficiaries to re-enter society and return to gainful employment. Frequently those rehabilitated are reunited with their families and continue their usual responsibilities. The work therapy program of the center includes the collection and repair of discarded materials and the operation of Salvation Army Thrift Stores in which restored materials are sold at moderate prices. Proceeds from these stores assist in supporting the program of the Men's Social Service Centers.

MISSING PERSONS AND INQUIRY BUREAU: A world-wide tracing and locating service of The Salvation Army, the work of which is greatly facilitated because of the Army's international nature. In the United States the work is largely carried on through correspondence and advertisements in *The War Cry* and foreign language newspapers. The bureau serves as a clearing house for all inquiries originating within a territory, as well as those from any other part of the world. The service maintains confidentiality and attempts to restore communication between individuals who mutually desire it.

MOBILE CANTEEN: A vehicle designed for the preparation and distribution of food and equipped to meet other needs in an emergency and disaster situation.

THE NATIONAL COMMANDER: President of all Salvation Army Corporations in the U.S.A.; chairman of the Commissioners' Conference; official representative of The Salvation Army to national organizations and at national functions.

NATIONAL HEADQUARTERS: Located in New York City, provides consultation services in the areas of Women's and Children's work, Welfare, Christian Education, Armed Forces, National Information and Women's Organizations within The Salvation Army, and is also the coordinating office for the entire country.

NEIGHBORHOOD VISITATION: House-to-house visitation by Salvationists who endeavor to bring help and spiritual counsel to those visited, particularly to individuals who are unable to attend a place of worship, or who have no church affiliation.

NURSES' FELLOWSHIP: An international organization within The Salvation Army inaugurated in 1943, designed to unite Salvationist and Christian nurses with leaders in the bonds of faith and fellowship by personal contact and correspondence.

OFFICER: A Salvationist engaged in full-time service as a duly accredited and ordained minister of religion in that branch of the Christian church known as The Salvation Army.

OUTPOST: An extension of The Salvation Army corps, usually in a new or remote area.

PERIODICALS: The *War Cry, Young Soldier,* and *All the World,* plus a number of additional publications of The Salvation Army issued for use within and without the organization.

SALVATIONIST: A lay member or officer of The Salvation Army.

SELF-DENIAL EFFORT: An annual observance during Holy Week characterized by prayer and a fund-raising project conducted by soldiers and friends of The Salvation Army, the proceeds of which are used in furthering the Army's missionary program throughout the world.

SERVICE EXTENSION PROGRAM: Maintained in rural areas, as well as in more populous districts, in which there is no established Salvation Army center of work. Each service unit is operated by The Army in cooperation with a local committee of representative citizens. Decisions as to general type of aid, areas of need, and administration methods are made by the committees in keeping with general Salvation Army policy. Field service is provided for the local Service Extension units, and the Divisional Headquarters acts as liaison between individual units and The Salvation Army's network of state-wide and interstate services.

SERVICES TO THE AGING: These include a variety of services benefiting individuals usually 65 years of age or over.

SINGING COMPANY A character-building activity within The Salvation Army for children 8 through 14 years of age who receive vocal instruction and function as a group.

SOCIAL WELFARE SERVICES DEPARTMENTS (attached to headquarters): Casework services available to needy persons irrespective of race or creed, including marital counseling and assistance in meeting problems arising from child-parent relationship, unmarried parenthood, physical and mental illness, poor housing, unemployment, old age and emotional maladjustment.

SOLDIER: A lay member of The Salvation Army who subscribes to the doctrines, beliefs and methods of the organization and who, without remuneration, gives all possible time in furthering the Army's purposes.

SONGSTER BRIGADE: An organized group of adult Salvationists who receive group vocal instruction and sing together to further the purposes of The Salvation Army. The brigade also serves as a character-building activity for implementing Army work with adults and older youth through the universally attractive medium of music.

SUNBEAMS: A division of the Salvation Army Girl Guards organized for girls from 6 through 10 years of age who subscribe to a program which promotes good character and good citizenship; develops proficiency and skills in subjects related to the care and development of the body, mind, soul and in service to others; emphasizes Christian living.

SUNDAY SCHOOL: A department of The Salvation Army corps that meets each Sunday for the purpose of educating attendants in the truths of the Bible and in Christian living, thus aiding in their spiritual development. Bible lessons are taught at the interest level of age groups from infancy to adulthood. Opportunities are also given for worship and fellowship periods.

TERRITORIAL COMMANDER: An officer of The Salvation Army directing a territory (region).

TERRITORY: A stated number of Salvation Army divisions in any one region or country.

THE SALVATION ARMY: The Salvation Army, founded in 1865, is an international religious and charitable movement organized and operated on a military pattern, and is a branch of the Christian church. The motivation of the organization is love for God and a practical concern for the needs of humanity. This is expressed by a spiritual ministry, the purposes of which are to preach the Gospel of Jesus Christ, disseminate Christian truths, provide personal counseling, and undertake the spiritual, moral and physical rehabilitation of all persons in need regardless of race or creed who come within its sphere of influence. These purposes are embodied in the certificates of incorporation in various Salvation Army corporations operative throughout the country. To carry out its purpose, The Salvation Army has established a widely diversified program of religious and social welfare services which are designed to meet the needs of children, youth and adults in all age groups.

TORCHBEARERS: A group within The Salvation Army corps or community center for all young people from 15 to 30 years of age, which seeks to influence youth for good through a cultural, educational and recreational program incorporating character training and spiritual guidance.

TRANSIENT SERVICE: An emergency service extended through The Salvation Army corps or welfare department to non-residents of a community who are by reason of their status ineligible for certain tax-supported welfare assistance. Since such non-residents are transient, their problems are usually acute, and service generally includes food and shelter on a temporary basis, and counsel and guidance in facilitating the ultimate resolving of their problems.

VACATION BIBLE SCHOOLS: Local corps educational programs of The Salvation Army for children (usually conducted for 10 to 14 day periods during the summer months) the purpose of which is fourfold: to provide a daily program for out-of-school children; to give additional Christian education; to reach young people with no church affiliation; and to win young people for Christ. Group participation, music and recreation are included in the curriculum.

VOLUNTEER ACTIVITIES: Wherever there is both a need and an opportunity for volunteer assistance in Salvation Army work, there are volunteer activities which aid in the extension of Salvation Army service in the community. Volunteer workers, who may be housewives, business and professional men and women, employed persons willing to share leisure time, as well as Salvation Army lay personnel, engage in many activities on behalf of needy and shut-in persons.

"FIRSTS" OF THE SALVATION ARMY IN PUERTO RICO AND THE VIRGIN ISLANDS

ADVISORY BOARD CHAIRMAN	William A. Waymouth
AUXILIARY, WOMEN'S	San Juan, 1969
AUXILIARY MEMBER	Mayoress Dona Felisa Rincon de Gautier
AUXILIARY PRESIDENT	Mrs. Jaime Sitiriche
BAND, INSTRUMENTAL	Caparra Temple, 1964 Academia William Booth Captain David Hepburn, Director
BUILDING CONSTRUCTED	Ponce
CHRISTMAS BASKET	Ponce, 1962
CHRISTMAS KETTLE EFFORT	Ponce, 1962
CONVERT	Israel Irrizary
CORPS	Caparra Temple, Nov. 16, 1961
CORPS (second)	San Juan Temple, Jan. 15, 1962
CORPS (third)	Ponce Temple, Aug. 15, 1962
CORPS CADET	Radames Hernandez
CORPS CADET BRIGADE	Ponce
CORPS CADET GRADUATE	Radames Hernandez, Nov., 1975
CORPS CADET RALLY	1972 (Ponce)
CORPS COLOR SERGEANT	Juan Batista, San Juan, 1965
CORPS OFFICERS	Capt. and Mrs. Richard Shaffstall
CORPS SECRETARY	Julio Santiago, San Juan, 1964
CORPS SERGEANT-MAJOR	Benjamin Pastrana, Caparra Terrace, 1964
CORPS TREASURER	Antonio Rodriguez Colon, Ponce, 1971
CORRECTIONAL SERVICES DIRECTOR	Ramon Vasquez, 1975
COUNCILS, YOUTH	1969
DAILY VACATION BIBLE SCHOOL	1968
DISASTER SERVICE WORK	1969

FUTURE OFFICERS' FELLOWSHIP SEMINAR	1968
GIRL GUARD TROOP	Ponce
HOME LEAGUE	Caparra Temple
HOME LEAGUE CAMP	1967
HOME LEAGUE FLAG	1968
HOME LEAGUE SECRETARY	Mrs. Carmen Nieves
HOTEL, MEN'S	Ponce, 1962
LEAGUE OF MERCY	Ponce, 1962 and 1963
MEETING, HOLINESS	Nov. 19, 1961, Caparra Temple
MEETING, MONDAY NIGHT AT THE TEMPLE	San Juan Temple (Regional) Nov. 10, 1975
MEETING, OPEN AIR	Nov. 19, 1961
MEETING, PRAYER	Nov. 16, 1961, Kindergarten Room, Academia William Booth, Caparra Terrace
MEETING, PUBLIC	Nov. 19, 1961
MEETING, SALVATION	Nov. 19, 1961
MEETING, SUNDAY SCHOOL	Nov. 19, 1961
OFFICER, COMMISSIONED	Mrs. Lieutenant Miguel Lopez
REGIONAL COMMANDER	Sr.-Major Tobias Martinez with Mrs. Martinez
SCHOOL	Academia William Booth, Caparra Terrace
SCHOOL (second)	Academia William Booth Ponce, Sept. 3, 1963
SCHOOL FOR OFFICERS' TRAINING	(Extension) San Juan, 1969
SELF-DENIAL INGATHERING	April 29, 1963
SERVICE UNIT COMMITTEE	1974
SERVICE UNIT REGIONAL DIRECTORY	Captain Samuel Eliasen, 1974
SINGING COMPANY	Caparra Temple, 1964 Mrs. Captain David Hepburn (Daisy)
SOLDIER, JUNIOR	Eric Diaz; Margaret Markham; Lorena Markham

SOLDIER, SENIOR	Mrs. B. Markham
SPIRITUAL CRUSADE	Cristo para el Mundo, 1966
SUMMER YOUTH TEAM	1968, David Appleby, Director
SUNBEAM TROOP	Caparra Temple, San Jose, San Juan Temple, 1970
WELFARE SERVICES DEPARTMENT	San Juan
WELFARE SERVICES DIRECTOR	Captain Cesar Ferri
WELFARE SERVICES WORKER	Mrs. Elsa Berghy, San Juan

OFFICERS STATIONED IN PUERTO RICO

Regional Commanders (in chronological order)
Sr. Major and Mrs. Tobias Martinez
Brigadier and Mrs. W. Eldred Churchill
Major and Mrs. Paul D. Seiler
Major and Mrs. Arnold Castillo
Brigadier and Mrs. Lawrence Pickering
Major and Mrs. Ralph Leidy
Brigadier and Mrs. William Hazzard

All Other Officers (in alphabetical order by rank)
Brigadier Freda Weatherly
Major and Mrs. Mario Jourdan
Major Aina Pettersson
Major and Mrs. Richard Shaffstall
Major and Mrs. Bernard Smith
Captain Frederick Damery
Captain and Mrs. Eric Diaz
Captain and Mrs. Samuel Eliasen
Captain and Mrs. Cesar Ferri
Captain and Mrs. Fidel Gonzalez
Captain Judith Heatherington
Captain and Mrs. David Hepburn
Captain Gilberta Hess
Captain and Mrs. Enrique Lalut
Captain and Mrs. Roberto Pagan
Captain and Mrs. Frank Payton
Lieutenant George Gomez
Lieutenant and Mrs. Felipe Machado
Lieutenant and Mrs. Douglas Marti
Lieutenant and Mrs. Victor Ortiz
Lieutenant Margaret Reed
Lieutenant Carol Snyder
Lieutenant and Mrs. Eduardo Suarez

Cadet-Lieutenant and Mrs. John Rondon
Auxiliary-Captain and Mrs. Juan J. Basualdo
Auxiliary-Captain and Mrs. Ruben Rodriquez
Auxiliary-Captain and Mrs. Enrique Vega
Envoy and Mrs. Walter Lopez

November, 1976

BIBLIOGRAPHY

James A. Bough and Roy C. Macridis, *Virgin Islands, America's Caribbean Outpost* (Walter F. Williams Publishing Co., 1970).

Paul J. Carlson, Col., Puerto Rico Report, unpublished, Oct. 2, 1961.

Isaac Dookhan, *A History of the Virgin Islands of the United States* (Caribbean Universities Press-Bowker Publishing Co., 1974).

Here's How: St. Thomas and St. John, (Here's How, 1975).

Randall Koladis and Mary Ann Todd, *St. Thomas on Foot and by Car*, (Koladis and Todd, 1972).

Alfredo Lopez, *The Puerto Rican Papers — Notes on the Re-emergence of a Nation* (N.Y. Bobbs Merrill & Co., 1973).

T. Herbert Martin, Puerto Rico Report, unpublished, 1965.

Tobias Martinez, Major, Puerto Rico Survey, unpublished, Dec. 3, 1955.

Tobias Martinez, Sr.-Major, Puerto Rico Survey, unpublished, 1961.

Gaetano Massa and Jose Louis Vivas, *The History of Puerto Rico* (Las Americas Publishing Co., 1970).

Paul D. Seiler, Major, Puerto Rico Report, unpublished, March, 1966.

William Slater, Col., Puerto Rico Report, unpublished, July 21, 1961.

H. Stimson, Col., Puerto Rico Report, unpublished, July 21, 1961.

Commonwealth of Puerto Rico, Economic Development and Ministry, Statement, 1974.

Puerto Rican Living, (San Juan, Living, Inc., 1973).

The Puerto Rican Experience, (N.Y. Littlefield, Adams & Co., 1973).

The War Cry (Chicago, Magazine, The Salvation Army, 1962-74).

The Year Book, (London, The Salvation Army, 1962-74).

Visitors' Guide to Puerto Rico (1973).

All else is primary source material, the author given access to all relevant material in Territorial and Regional Headquarters files, and permitted to correspond with officers who are or have been stationed on the Puerto Rican field, laity and other interested persons. Many personal interviews were conducted. Tapes were contributed by David and Daisy Hepburn, Captain and Mrs. Enrique Lalut, Major and Mrs. Frank Payton, Major and Mrs. Richard Shaffstall, Mrs. Albertina Skatliffe and Mrs. Gilberta Hess Valentin.

INDEX

Academia Rovira, 23-25
Academia William Booth (see also Academia Rovira), Rio Piedras, 25-29, 37, 40, 47-48, 50, 53-56, 65, 74, 109; Ponce, 56, 60, Aibonito, 72, 78, 107
Airall, Cadet, 83
Agrelot, Jose Miguel, 54
Allemand, Carlos, 112, 113-114
Allemand, Mrs. Carlos (Emma), 112, 113
Alvarez, Mrs., 111
Appleby, David, 50, 78
Archibald, Sister Doris, 85
Arecibo, 97

Baker, Agnes, 82-83
Band, 30, 50, 54, 78, 82-83, 105, 111, 113, 131
Baranquitas, 29
Barcelo, Mayor, 69
Barkey, Robert, 27
Basualdo, Sergeant and Mrs. Juan Jose, 113
Batista, Color Sergeant Angel, 101
Bayamon, 80, 101
Bennazar, Antonio, 30
Bishop, R., 83
Blynden, Corps Cadet Guardian, 84
Booth, William, 31, 100, 131
Borrero, Sr. Victor, 118
Bosio, Pedro Javier, 31
Branch, Sister, 84
Breckenridge, James D.C., 31
Brindley, Gayle, 71, 72

Brooks, Sister, 85
Burgos, Pedro, 31

Caguas, 80, 97
Camp, 65, 72, 78, 80, 97, 107
Campbell, Reverend Donald, 71
Caparra Temple Corps Community Center, 37, 38, 43, 50, 53, 55, 63, 65, 67, 72, 74, 79, 104-105
Caparra Terrace, 24, 26, 28, 38, 40, 43, 47, 48, 55, 67, 80
Caparra Terrace Academy, see Academia William Booth
Caparra Terrace Corps, see Caparra Temple Corps Community Center
Capo, Nivea, 49
Caribbean School (see also Academia William Booth at Ponce), 60
Carlisle, Mrs. Harry, 79
Carlson, Paul J., 25, 26, 66, 111
Carlson, Mrs. 71
Castaneda, Reverend, 50
Castillo, Arnold, 54, 56, 66, 67, 73, 77, 78, 79
Castillo, Mrs. Arnold, 56, 67, 73, 77-80
Cayey, 97
Central America and West Indies Territory, 13, 14, 22
Charlotte-Amalie Corps, 82-86, 101
Chesham, Howard, 71, 132
Chesham, Mrs. Howard, vii, 132

155 . . .

Cholito, Don, see Jose Miguel Agrelot
Churchill, Eldred, 40, 41, 46, 47, 50, 64, 73, 75, 78, 109, 114
Churchill, Mrs. Eldred, 40, 41, 46, 50, 67, 73, 109, 114
Cintron, Mayor Juan H., 71
Colon, Fernando, 66, 71
Colon, Ramon, 102
Colon, Victor, 21
Corps Cadet program, 76-77, 80, 83, 100, 131-132
Council of Evangelical Churches, The, 19
Coutts, Frederick, v, 54
Cowan, Llewellyn, 20
Cox, Shirley, 88
Cuba, Joe, 102
Culshaw, Owen, 22

Davila, Luis, 72, 106-107
Davila, Mrs. Luis (Carmen), 72, 106-107
De La Rosa, Iris, 39, 101
De La Rosa, Jose, 39, 101
Del Valle, Corps Sergeant-Major Isaac, 39, 101
Del Valle, Margarita, 39
Diaz, Eric, 43, 44, 80, 102-103
Diaz, Mrs. Eric, 80
Diaz, Ramon, 43, 44
Ditmer, Stanley, 71
Dodd, Charles, 15-16

Eastern School for Officers' Training, 43
Elderly, see Golden-Age Program
Eliasen, Hjalmar, 31
Eliasen, Samuel, 67, 71, 85, 131
Evans, Dr. Melvin H., 88

Fabio, Flag Sergeant, 84
Fabio, Sister, 84
Ferre, Governor Luis A., 71
Ferri, Cesar, 72, 80, 110

Ferri, Mrs., 110
Figueroa, Ruben O., 31
Fourquet Jr., Hernan, 80, 112-113
Fourquet, Mrs. Hernan, 80, 101-102
Fowler, Bruce, 110
French, Holland, 30
Future Officers' Fellowship, 100

Garcia, Teddy, 50
Garner, Louis, 72
General, the, 14, 16, 17
Girl Guards, 52, 102
Golden-Age Program, 60-61
Gonzales, Danilo, 48, 50
Gonzales, Fidel, 64, 72, 111
Gonzales, Mrs. Fidel, 72
Gonzales, Pedro A., 18
Graham, Billy, 55
Grandstand, 97, 116, 119, 121
Grayber, Dr. G., 72
Guauate, 110
Guayama, 80, 97, 99, 101, 110, 116-123
Guayama Corps Community Center, 116-123
Guerra, E. Combas, 31
Guerrero, Raul, 89

Hamalainen, Markku, 71, 111
Hansen, Mrs. Betty, 48
Harbor Light Corps program, 25
Harris, Colonel William, 23-24
Hatt, Gunter, 31
Hawkins, Iris, 82, 85
Hazzard, William, 73, 85, 100, 131
Hazzard, Mrs. William, 73, 85, 100, 131
Headstart, 51, 52
Hepburn, Samuel, 16
Hepburn, David, 47-52, 54-58, 67
Hepburn, Mrs. David (Daisy), 47-49, 51-52, 56-58, 67
Hernandez, Angelina, 98-99, 132
Hess, Gilbert and Mrs., 115

Hess, Gilberta, 43-47, 62, 63, 110, 114-116
Hodges, Mrs. Mai, 82, 88
Holder, G., 83
Holman, Aaron, 30
Holz, Ernest and Mrs., 71
Home League, 100, 111; Bayamon, 81; Caparra Terrace, 29, 41, 49, 52-53, 74; Grandstand, 119; Guayama, 121; La Perla, 67, 102, 104; Loiza, 106, 107, 108; Ponce, 63, 64, 111; St. Thomas, 85; San Jose, 115, 116; San Juan Temple, 72, 74, 101, 102
Hope House-Multiplex Welfare Center, 37-38, 56, 73, 78, 80, 109-110, 112
Hotel (Ponce), 59, 60
Huber, Miss Lydia, 74
Humacao, 97

International College for Officers, 65, 112
International Headquarters, 14, 15, 17

Jamaica, Kingston, 22
James, Sister, 85-86
Jimenez, Ing. Jorge J., 31
Jimenez, Miguel A., 21
Johnson, Rev. Donald E., 30
Jourdan, Mario, 85
Jourdan, Mrs. Mario, 85, 131
Junior Legion, 42, 62, 74
Junior Soldier, 14, 30, 44, 63, 83, 100
Jusino, Corps Cadet Marta, 113, 131

Kitching, Wilfred, 30

La Perla, x, 39, 41-43, 66-70, 73, 74, 78, 80, 97, 101, 102-104, 109, 116

Lalut, Enrique, 48, 53-54, 64, 67-70, 73
Lalut, Mrs. Enrique (Brenda), 58, 64, 67-70, 73
Lanauze, Mrs. Estela Maria Davila, 31
Laporte, Corps Cadet Benson, 111
Lastra, Dr. Carlos J., 31, 55
League of Mercy, 97, 101; Grandstand, 119; Ponce, 59; St. Croix, 85; San Juan-La Perla, 46, 104; San Juan Temple, 73
Leidy, Ralph, 73, 80, 105, 111, 118
Leidy, Mrs. Ralph, 73, 80, 111
Leland, Brenda, see Mrs. Enrique (Brenda) Lalut
Lesprance, Cadet, 83
Lochart, Alfred, 85
Loiza, 72, 80, 97, 101, 105-109
Loiza Corps Community Center, 80, 106-109
Lopez, Miguel and Mrs., 49
Lugo, Dr. Samuel E., 21, 30
Lugo, Mrs. Samuel E., 30

McIntyre, J. Joseph, 31
McNally, Robert and Mrs., 53
Machado, Franklin, 110
Machado, Felipe, 116-123
Machado, Mrs. Felipe (Daisy), 116-122
Maldonado, A.W., 31
Maldonado, Rev. Raphael Angel, 31
Manhattan Citadel New York corps, 43, 50, 78
Manneke, Mrs., 83
Manwaring, Mrs. Weldon, 79-80
Marklen, Mai, see Mrs. Mai Hodges
Marshall, Norman, 14-15
Marti, Douglas and Zaida, 80-81
Martin, T. Herbert, 74-75, 78
Martin, Mrs. T. Herbert, 74

Martinez, Jesus, 50
Martinez, Mrs. Tobias, 14, 16, 38, 39-40, 73
Martinez, Mrs. Peter, 79
Martinez, Tobias, v, 13-27, 30, 38, 39-40, 73, 75, 109
Martinez, Virginia, 38
Marzan, Mrs. Carmen, 39
Mayaguez, 75, 78, 80, 97, 110
Mayaguez Corps, 75, 78, 80
Melendez, Medarda, 41
Mendez, Commandante Ernesto Lugo, 30
Mendez, Hector, 55
Mendez, Mrs. Hector, see Milagros Pagan
Mendez, Pedro, 71
Men's Fellowship Club, 101
Mercer, Corps Sergeant-Major, 84
Modeste, Hector, 31
Monacillo, 49, 50-51
Monet, Mr. and Mrs., 46-47
Montilla, Colonel Rafael, 31
Morris, Captain, 85
Multiplex Welfare Center, see Hope House-Multiplex Welfare Center

National Headquarters, 14, 21, 23
Neild, Mrs. Philip, 79
New York School for Officers' Training, 47, 50, 64, 79, 100; Puerto Rico extension, 71, 79, 100, 108, 111, 122
Noce, Chaplain William S., 31

Old San Juan, xi, 13, 24, 25, 30, 37, 39, 41, 70, 71, 97, 109
Oliveras, Ex. Teniente Alejandro, 31
Olsen, Sally, 53
Ongay, Miss Carmen, 30
Operation Sharing, 49
Ortiz, Victor, 72, 80, 104-107, 123, 131

Ortiz, Mrs. Victor (Sara), 80, 104-107, 123
Oso Blanco, 110
Owen, Ray, 98

Pagan, Roberto, 42, 54, 65-66, 71, 72, 109, 111, 112, 113, 118
Pagan, Enrique, 101
Pagan, Milagros, 43, 55
Pagan, Mrs. Roberto, 42, 65-67, 72, 112
Pagan, Yufo, 48
Page, Clyde, 19
Palma, Mr. Agustin Vera, 30
Parlack, Mrs., 84
Pastrana, Benjamin, 50
Payton, Frank, 41, 42, 58, 61-66, 67, 79
Payton, Mrs. Frank, 41, 58, 61-65, 67
Pelley, Mr. and Mrs., 27
Pepper, Albert, 43
Petra, Dona, 114
Pickering, Lawrence K., 71, 73, 79, 111
Pickering, Mrs. Lawrence K., 72, 73, 79
Pimentel, Carmen, see Mrs. Luis Davila
Pizarro, Mrs. Yolanda, 107, 108-109
Pizarro, Yolanda and Ivett, 108
Phillips, M., 84
Plaza Colon, 13, 38
Ponce, 28, 29, 43, 47, 56, 58-66, 71, 101, 110-114
Ponce, school, see Academia William Booth at Ponce
Ponce Advisory Board, 64-65, 77
Ponce Corps Community Center, 53, 61-64, 65-66, 71, 111, 112-114
Princessa, 110
Puerto Rico Youth Council, 53

Punta Lima, 110
Pullen, Mrs. Webster, 40
Pullen, Webster, 21

Regional Headquarters, 37, 40, 65, 73-81, 85, 89, 97, 100, 101, 111
Reyes, Baldomera, 21
Rincon de Gautier, Dona Felisa, 14, 19-20, 31, 56, 97, 109
Rio Piedras, 24, 48, 65, 101, 104-105, 109
Robinson, Chaplain (Major) Richard E., 31
Rodriguez, Elvin, 72
Rodriquez, Rev. Antonio Rivera, 30
Rodriquez, Ruben and Josefina, 105, 121
Rosas, Ledo Juvenla, 31
Rouse, Mrs. Geraldine, 87-88
Rovira-Sanchez, Eduardo, 99-100

St. Croix, 85, 87-89, 97, 101
St. John, 87
St. Thomas, 81-87, 101
SAYSO, 78, 79
San Jose, 114-116
San Jose Corps, 63, 80, 105, 114-116
San Juan, x-58, 70, 71, 72, 79, 101, 111, 131
San Juan Advisory Board, 40, 54, 56, 74, 75, 77
San Juan-La Perla Corps Community Center, 102-104
San Juan Slum Project, 67-68
San Juan Temple Corps Community Center, 30, 37, 40-42, 53, 65, 67, 71, 72, 74, 101-102, 105, 109, 114, 122
San Juan Women's Auxiliary, 79-80
Sanchez, Reverend Gildo, 31
Sandells, George, 13-14
Santana, Benjamin, 21

Santiago, Ephraim, 79
Santiago, Julio, 21, 105
Santiago, Mrs. Petra, 21
Santiago, Samuel J. Velez, 21
Santiago, William Fred, 21
Scatliffe, Albertina, 82, 83
School for Officers' Training, see New York School for Officers' Training
Seiler, Paul D., 73, 75, 77, 89
Seiler, Paul Sr., 54
Shaffstall, 26-30, 42-43, 47, 59-61, 71, 112
Shaffstall, Mrs., 26, 27, 28, 42-43, 47, 59
Shaffstall, Richard and Eric, 26, 27
Shennan, Minnie Belle, 71
Sitiriche, Mrs. Jaime, 79
Slater, 24
Smith, Bernard, 38-41, 54, 67, 78-79
Smith, Mrs. Bernard, 38, 39
Smith, Eugenie, 84
Smith, Young People's Sergeant-Major, 84
Snyder, Carol, 43, 45-47
South America East Territory, 15
Sparks, Herbert, 26-27
Stannard, John, 14, 88
Steele, Agnes, 84
Stimson, Colonel, 24, 25
Suarez, Miguel, 111
Suarez, Moises and Mrs., 72
Sunbeams, 80, 106, 107, 108, 110

Territorial Headquarters, 20, 31, 75
Thomas, Commanding Sergeant and Mrs. Evan, 85
Tobin, Cadet, 83
Todd, Brother and Sister, 84
Torchbearers, 45, 63, 104, 106, 108
Toro, Senador Arturo Ortiz, 30
Trotman, Adjutant, 82, 83

United Evangelical Church, 19
United Fund, 101
United Home League, 74
USA Eastern Territory, 22-23, 24, 25, 26, 48, 50, 56, 66, 71, 72, 75-81, 82, 101, 111, 118, 123, 132
USA Western Territory, 14, 16-17, 71

Valentin, Carlos, 114
Valentin, Mrs. Carlos, see Captain Gilberta Hess
Valez, Arlene, 107
Vassallo, Efrain, 71
Vasquez, Ramon, 45, 110

Vega, Auxiliary Captain, 105
Vega, Enrique, 104
Vega, Sergeant and Mrs. Enrique, 104-105
Velez de Perez, Mrs. Mercedes, 30
Virgin Islands, 81-87

Waldron, John, vii, 71
WAPA, 98, 133
War Cry, 71, 72, 101, 102, 111
Waymouth, William, 40
Weatherly, Freda, 28-29, 38, 40-41
White, Henry and Mrs., 59
Wiseman, Clarence D., 132
World Services Fund, 101
WOR-TV, 27

. . . 160